Designing Writing

A Practical Guide

Mike Palmquist
Colorado State University

Bedford / St. Martin's

Boston ◆ New York

For Bedford/St. Martin's

Executive Editor: Leasa Burton
Developmental Editor: Laura Arcari
Editorial Assistant: Maria Halovanic
Production Supervisor: Yexenia Markland
Project Management: Books By Design, Inc.
Senior Marketing Manager: Richard Cadman
Text Design: Claire Seng-Niemoeller
Cover Design: Donna Lee Dennison

Composition: Claire Seng-Niemoeller
Printing and Binding: Haddon Craftsmen, an RR Donnelley & Sons Company

President: Joan E. Feinberg
Editorial Director: Denise Wydra
Editor in Chief: Karen S. Henry
Director of Marketing: Karen Melton Soeltz
Director of Editing, Design, and Production: Marcia Cohen
Manager, Publishing Services: Emily Berleth

Library of Congress Catalog Card Number: 2004112880

Manufactured in the United States of America.

0   9   8   7   6   5

f   e   d   c   b   a

For information, write: Bedford/St. Martin's, 75 Arlington Street,
Boston, MA 02116   (617-399-4000)

ISBN: 0–312–45017–6
EAN: 978–0–312–45017–5

Acknowledgments

Acknowledgments and copyrights can be found at the back of the book on page 125, which constitutes a continuation of the copyright page.

Preface

Designing Writing is based on the premise that content might be king, but kings are at their best when they're appropriately attired. At the beginning of the twenty-first century, the best-dressed documents are those that most effectively draw the reader's eye to key ideas and information, help the reader understand complex concepts, and set an appropriate tone. Strong arguments, well-chosen support, and clear writing are critical to the success of documents. To ensure that documents are most effective, however, writers are reinterpreting and extending what the ancient rhetors called hypokrisis—the rhetorical canon of delivery.

Delivery includes such traditional concerns as the voice, tone, and style of a document. With growing frequency, however, modern writers are thinking of delivery in terms of documents' visual appearance and appeal. The growing importance of this visual aspect of rhetoric—which in this book is referred to as the design of a document—has paralleled the development of communication technologies that have simplified the tasks of composing and distributing documents. As writers have found it easier to share their documents with their intended readers, they've found significant competition for their attention. Long gone are the days when children understood the old joke about newspapers being "black and white and red all over." Instead, magazines and newspapers employ sophisticated mixes of photographs, images, tables and charts, and text formatting to

> *Long gone are the days when children understood the old joke about newspapers being "black and white and red all over."*

convey their messages; Web sites use images, animation, audio, and video to compete with each other for "eyeballs"; and even run-of-the-mill business reports rely heavily on sophisticated layout and design.

The challenge for writers and writing teachers is how best to attend to the design of a document without diverting attention from the other elements of a strong foundation: effective arguments, well-chosen support, and clear writing. *Designing Writing* takes up this challenge by considering document design as part of a writer's overall approach to creating a document. Rather than presenting document design as an add-on, something that's done only after the real work of composing a document has been completed, *Designing Writing* focuses on document design as part of the larger set of tools that writers can use to consider their audience and purpose and to adapt to the contexts in which their documents are written and read. *Designing Writing,* in short, treats document design as a rhetorical act.

Key Features

With annotated full-color illustrations throughout the text, *Designing Writing* literally shows students how to use the principles of visual rhetoric in their own writing. Part One, "Designing for Effect," illustrates how design works with writing to achieve a variety of purposes; Part Two, "Understanding Design Elements," introduces the basic elements of document design; and Part Three, "Designing Documents," guides students through the process of designing essays, articles, brochures, flyers, multimedia presentations, and Web sites.

Brief enough to be used as a supplement, *Designing Writing* offers thorough coverage of basic design principles in an extremely flexible format. Key features of this book include:

- An emphasis on rhetorical choices that writers make as they design documents
- Practical advice on creating a range of genres, from academic essays to brochures, Web sites, and PowerPoint presentations
- More than 60 full-color examples of visual documents
- How-to sidebars with illustrated step-by-step instructions for using basic computer tools to design documents
- Design activities that ask students both to analyze design choices and to practice making decisions about design (Parts One and Two)
- Guidelines and checklists for designing specific genres, including essays, articles, brochures, flyers, presentations, and Web sites (Part Three)

Designing Writing focuses on what writers need to know — how to analyze the visual principles that inform convincing documents and how to make effective choices as they design their own writing.

Acknowledgments

I am indebted to the reviewers who offered helpful suggestions about an early draft of the book: Mark Canada, University of North Carolina, Pembroke; Donna Halford, Texas A&M University, Kingsville; Scott Orme, Spokane Community College; Stephanie Paterson, California State University, Stanislaus; Rochelle Rodrigo, Mesa Community College; and Michelle Rogge Gannon, University of South Dakota.

I am particularly indebted to the student writers whose work I adapted from *The Bedford Researcher* for use in this book: Jenna Alberter, Aaron Batty, Gaele Lopez, Maria Sanchez-Traynor, and Rianne Uilk.

At Bedford/St. Martin's, I want to thank Joan Feinberg and Denise Wydra for asking me to take on this project and for supporting it so strongly as it was developed. Thanks to Leasa Burton for her editorial direction and in particular for her thoughtful suggestions and careful reviews. Leasa is the kind of editor with whom every writer should be fortunate to work. Thanks also to Laura Arcari for her developmental editing of this book and for her suggestions for its design activities, and to Maria Halovanic for her editorial support and general good humor under pressure. A big thank you to the production team, Emily Berleth and Nancy Benjamin, for guiding this complex project through the process with such professionalism. And many thanks to Claire Seng-Niemoeller for the book's superb design.

Most of all, I thank my family for supporting me as I worked on this project.

Mike Palmquist

Contents

Introduction

I magine books without page numbers, newspapers without headlines, magazines without color. Imagine Web sites without links and passports without photographs. Imagine a world where every document uses the same font, line spacing, and margins, and you can't judge a book by its cover because all the covers look alike.

It would be a world without document design. And frankly, it wouldn't be pretty.

Document design is the use of visual elements—fonts, colors, page layout, and illustrations—to enhance the effectiveness of written documents. The principles underlying document design can be particularly helpful when you want to convey complex ideas, information, or processes. For a reader, a well-designed table or chart can be far more effective at clarifying complex information than even the most eloquently written sentences. Similarly, a numbered or bulleted list can present the critical steps in a complicated process in a way that plain text can't. By understanding and applying the principles of document design, writers can make their documents easier to understand and easier to use.

Document design is also the basis of **visual rhetoric**, a term used to describe how visual elements work together in a document to persuade or convince a reader. The emotional impact of a well-chosen illustration, such as a photograph of a starving child or a video clip of aid workers rushing to help victims of a natural disaster, can do far more than words alone to persuade a reader to take action. Likewise, formatting text in a way that draws a reader's attention to a passage can help you highlight a key idea or concept. Using document design to enhance the persuasiveness of your document increases the likelihood that your readers will respond to your document in the manner you intend. That is, it can help you achieve your purposes as a writer.

> *The emotional impact of a well-chosen illustration . . . can do far more than words alone to persuade a reader to take action.*

Designing Writing shows you how to use document design principles and elements to create effective, usable documents. This book has three parts:

- Part One, Designing for Effect, explains how design principles can help you achieve your purposes as a writer, meet your readers' needs and interests, adapt to the settings in which your document will be read, and work with sources.
- Part Two, Understanding Design Elements, discusses the key elements of document design: fonts, line spacing, and alignment; page layout; navigation aids for print and digital documents; color, shading, borders, and rules; and illustrations.
- Part Three, Designing Documents, explores the design characteristics of six common documents: essays, articles, brochures, flyers, multimedia presentations, and Web sites.

As you read *Designing Writing*, you'll find clear explanations of important design concepts and techniques, a wealth of illustrations, and step-by-step "how-to" instructions for using the design tools in your word processor. Parts One and Two also contain end-of-chapter activities that will help you gain a better understanding of the design principles and elements discussed in this book. Each of these features is crafted to help you use the principles and elements of good document design. The "how-to" instructions focus on the features provided by Microsoft Word because Word is widely used in the Windows and Macintosh worlds, most word processing programs use commands similar to those found in Word, and length considerations made it impractical to provide detailed step-by-step instructions for other word processing software.

A key concept running through *Designing Writing* is that document design isn't something that is applied to a document only after it is written. Instead, it's something you should consider throughout your composing process, from your first attempts to generate ideas for a topic to your final efforts to edit your draft. By thinking visually—that is, by thinking as a document designer—you can create documents that are more effective and usable than those that rely on words alone.

PART ONE

Designing
for Effect

An effective document is easy to understand and easy to use. It makes its point clearly and persuasively. Creating an effective document begins with a series of questions about the writing situation in which you and your readers will find yourselves: What is my purpose? Who are my readers? Why are they reading my document? What do they know about my topic? How will their experiences affect their reading of my document? Where will they read my document? In what medium—on paper or on screen—will they read the document? The answers to these questions will influence not only what you write but how you present your writing to your readers.

The most important factor in the success of your writing project is, without question, the ability to express your ideas and arguments clearly. Clearly written prose, however, is not always enough to help you achieve your purposes as a writer. In many cases, you need to consider how your document's design will affect your readers.

Consider the difference between an article that is designed like a typical college essay and an article designed for a magazine. Look at Figures A and B. The text in the two articles is identical, but the magazine article contains photographs, charts, and graphs that clarify the ideas and information in the text. The magazine article also uses headings, subheadings, and pull quotes—quotations pulled out of the text—to call readers' attention to important concepts in the article. Even the most dedicated readers (such as

Guess What F is For? Fat

By Claudia Wallis

The way state representative Gary Biggs sees it, things in Arkansas had pretty much reached critical mass. Not only were 60% of adults in the T state overweight or obese, but their kids were catching up fast. A quarter of Arkansas' high school students are overweight or "at risk." The state health director estimates that Type 2 diabetes, formerly known as the adult-onset variety, is up 800% in kids over the past decade. Even the state's preschoolers have grown shockingly plump: almost 10% are overweight. Says Biggs: "I have been on the house public-health committee for three terms, and I got tired of hearing "Thank God for Mississippi"—which has an even higher obesity rate than Arkansas does. Something had to be done.

Something was. As the state's 1,139 public schools opened their doors for a new year, they faced a new task. For the first time they will be asked to issue a body mass index, or BMI. As lawmakers initially envisioned the plan when they passed the Biggs-sponsored bill in April, schools were to literally add a section to report cards—alongside the traditional assessments in reading, writing and 'rithmetic—for this measure of a child's body. At a time when schools are increasingly taking on responsibilities once left to parents—from teaching about sex and drugs to enforcing dress codes—this development was perhaps not all that surprising. But feeding a child is arguably a parent's most elementary task, so the prospect of school's intruding in such an intimate matter and issuing F-is-for-fat grades was mortifying to some.

"There was concern among some parents of overweight children that the report would be snatched from the child's hand and passed around for everyone to see, and the child would be tormented," explains state PTA president Kathy McFetridge. So last week Arkansas' new child-

health advisory committee voted to modify the plan. Health reports will be mailed separately to parents, and family may even opt out of the program. In addition, chastened policy makers agreed to begin pilots of the policy in a few schools this fall before rolling it out statewide in the spring.

Arkansas is the first state to embrace, however gingerly, the health-report-card approach, but other states are exploring similar policies and other steps to control childhood obesity. They are propelled by some remarkably scary statistics. Nationally, 15% of children ages 5 to 19 are overweight, triple the rate of 20 years ago. Research suggests that fat adolescents have a 70% to 80% chance of becoming fat adults. They face higher rates of atherosclerosis, hypertension and diabetes. "These kids could need coronary bypass in their 20s," says Kelly Brownell, director of the Yale University Center for Eating and Weight Disorders. "This could be the first generation of American children to lead shorter lives than their parents."

The medical community has been sounding the alarm for several years. Just last month, the American Academy of Pediatrics (A.A.P.) formally recommended that doctors make BMI assessments a routine part of annual physicals. No one doubts that the pediatrician's office belongs on the front lines of confronting the epidemic, but is school the right place to fight this battle? And can weigh-ins at the nurse's office be helpful without causing a lot of collateral damage to tender egos?

Many obesity experts argue that the lunchroom and gym are the spots where schools should focus their energies. "Are we offering enough P.E. classes? How do we get more nutritious lunch meals into schools? How do we promote a healthy, active lifestyle without stigmatizing overweight children?" asks Dr. Nancy Krebs, a University of Colorado pediatrician

Figure A Article in a format typically used for academic essays. Information is provided through double-spaced text with one-inch margins. (*Source: Time*, September 15, 2003, pp. 68–69)

Figure B The same article formatted for publication in a magazine. Photographs, colors, charts, and font formatting call attention to and convey key information in the article. (*Source: Time,* September 15, 2003, pp. 68–69)

writing instructors) are likely to find the magazine-formatted version of the article more interesting and attractive.

Although the article formatted for publication in a magazine is more attractive and does a better job of calling attention to key ideas and information, few writing instructors would welcome an essay that is formatted like an article in a magazine. The design features of most academic essays—wide margins, double-spacing, easy-to-read fonts—make it easier for instructors and peers to read and comment on a text. When there are no spaces for handwritten notes, the document is less useful for its intended audience of writing instructors.

So what should you do? One approach is to consider how some of the design elements found in an effective magazine article might be used in an academic essay. Figure C, on the following page, shows a third version of the essay in Figures A and B. Notice how it uses colors, photographs, pull quotes, and sidebars to call readers' attention to important ideas while still retaining the elements of an academic essay that make it easier for instructors to jot down comments on the document.

Learn about using color on p. 66, illustrations on p. 77, pull quotes on p. 54, and sidebars on p. 56.

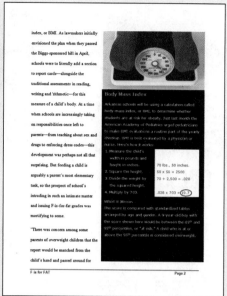

Figure C Article using design elements common in academic essays and magazines. The same article shown in Figures A and B incorporating design elements from academic and magazine layouts. (*Source: Time,* September 15, 2003, pp. 68–69)

Designing for effect means considering how the document design principles of balance, emphasis, placement, repetition, and consistency can help you achieve your purposes as a writer, meet the expectations of your readers, adapt to the constraints of genre (type of document) and medium (print or digital), use evidence from your sources, and identify your sources. As you design your document, keep two additional principles in mind: moderation and simplicity. Using visual elements excessively can work against the effectiveness and usability of a document. Documents that use an overwhelming mix of design elements — color, illustrations, fonts — can obscure important ideas and information. Using design elements moderately to create simple yet effective designs is the best approach to document design.

CHAPTER 1

Understanding Design Principles

Before you begin formatting text and inserting illustrations, think carefully about how the design of your document can help you accomplish your goals as a writer. As you reflect on potential designs, consider how those designs will affect the clarity, persuasiveness, attractiveness, and ease of use of your document. Keep the following important design principles in mind:

- **Balance**—the vertical and horizontal alignment of elements on your pages
- **Emphasis**—the placement and formatting of elements, such as headings and subheadings, so they catch your reader's attention
- **Placement**—the location of elements on your pages
- **Repetition**—the use of elements, such as headers and footers, navigation menus, and page numbers, across the pages in your document
- **Consistency**—the extent to which you format and place text and illustrations the same way throughout your document

1a Achieving Balance . . . or Not

Balance refers to the symmetry of elements on your pages. Depending on your document, you might adopt a symmetrical design, where elements are centered or justified (aligned along both the right and left margins), or an asymmetrical design, where elements are not evenly balanced across the page (see Figure 1.1). Although most writers think of balance and symmetry in terms of the horizontal alignment of text and images on a page (left, center, right, justified), you will see some documents that are balanced vertically as well (top, bottom; see Figure 1.2).

Learn about aligning text on p. 40.

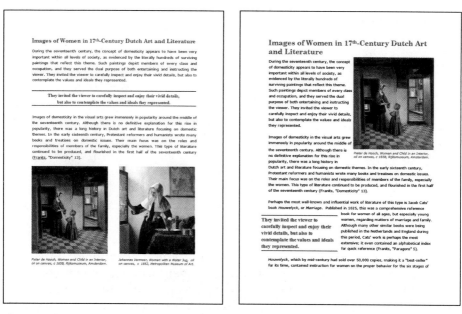

Figure 1.1 Symmetrical and asymmetrical layouts. Each of these layouts suggests a different sense of balance and movement. The symmetrical design (left) is balanced and restful. The asymmetrical design (right) is unbalanced and suggests movement across the page.

Figure 1.2 Symmetrical layout that also achieves vertical balance.

The type of balance you choose for your document will be influenced by the effect you want it to have on your readers. Symmetrical designs evoke a restful appearance, for example, whereas asymmetrical designs suggest movement. When looking at a symmetrical, or balanced, page design, the reader is likely to focus on a particular part of a document, such as a centrally placed image or heading. In contrast, when readers view a page with an asymmetrical, or unbalanced, design, their eyes move around the page from one element to the next. Research suggests that the gaze of North American, European, and Australian readers moves first from the upper left to the lower right regions of a page in a Z pattern before finally settling on a particular text passage, image, or heading. An asymmetrical design supports this pattern of eye moment, while a symmetrical design disrupts it, calling the reader's eyes to the center of the page.

Your writing situation also will influence your decisions about whether to use a balanced or unbalanced design. For example, documents such as legal notices, financial reports, and obituaries often use a balanced design to reflect writers' concerns about conveying a sense of seriousness and calm. In contrast, sales brochures, magazine ads, and movie posters often use an unbalanced design to reflect writers' interests in evoking a sense of excitement and anticipation.

1b Emphasizing Elements

If you want to call attention to something you are saying, you can raise your voice or change your tone. If you want to call attention to something you have written, you can format it in a way that draws the reader's eye. For example, you might use a different color to add emphasis to a heading or subheading, or you might place a border around an important paragraph. You can also call attention to a particular element—such as a heading, a paragraph, or an image—by making it look different from surrounding elements. You could, for example, change the font size, color, or border around a paragraph, thereby drawing the reader's eye to it.

You can also emphasize certain ideas and information in a document by using illustrations, such as a photograph, drawing, chart, or graph. The photograph and caption in Figure 1.3 emphasize an idea discussed in the surrounding paragraphs. Note how the placement of the photograph breaks up the text and catches the reader's attention. Because illustrations are often viewed first—and because readers sometimes fail to read the text associated with an illustration—it's important to choose illustrations carefully.

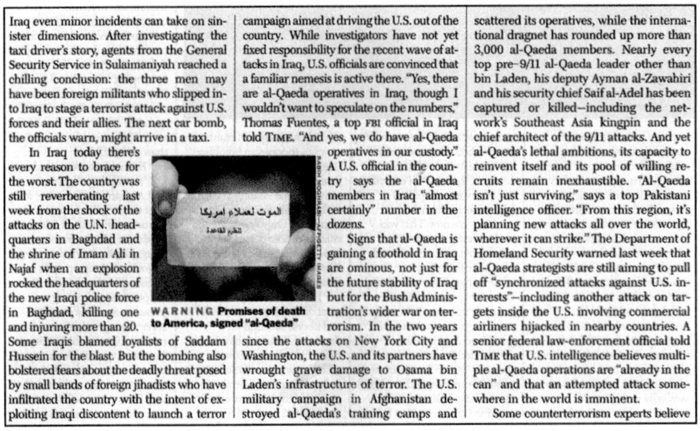
Iraq even minor incidents can take on sinister dimensions. After investigating the taxi driver's story, agents from the General Security Service in Sulaimaniyah reached a chilling conclusion: the three men may have been foreign militants who slipped into Iraq to stage a terrorist attack against U.S. forces and their allies. The next car bomb, the officials warn, might arrive in a taxi.

In Iraq today there's every reason to brace for the worst. The country was still reverberating last week from the shock of the attacks on the U.N. headquarters in Baghdad and the shrine of Imam Ali in Najaf when an explosion rocked the headquarters of the new Iraqi police force in Baghdad, killing one and injuring more than 20. Some Iraqis blamed loyalists of Saddam Hussein for the blast. But the bombing also bolstered fears about the deadly threat posed by small bands of foreign jihadists who have infiltrated the country with the intent of exploiting Iraqi discontent to launch a terror campaign aimed at driving the U.S. out of the country. While investigators have not yet fixed responsibility for the recent wave of attacks in Iraq, U.S. officials are convinced that a familiar nemesis is active there. "Yes, there are al-Qaeda operatives in Iraq, though I wouldn't want to speculate on the numbers," Thomas Fuentes, a top FBI official in Iraq told TIME. "And yes, we do have al-Qaeda operatives in our custody." A U.S. official in the country says the al-Qaeda members in Iraq "almost certainly" number in the dozens.

WARNING Promises of death to America, signed "al-Qaeda"

RABIH MOGHRABI—AFP/GETTY IMAGES

Signs that al-Qaeda is gaining a foothold in Iraq are ominous, not just for the future stability of Iraq but for the Bush Administration's wider war on terrorism. In the two years since the attacks on New York City and Washington, the U.S. and its partners have wrought grave damage to Osama bin Laden's infrastructure of terror. The U.S. military campaign in Afghanistan destroyed al-Qaeda's training camps and scattered its operatives, while the international dragnet has rounded up more than 3,000 al-Qaeda members. Nearly every top pre–9/11 al-Qaeda leader other than bin Laden, his deputy Ayman al-Zawahiri and his security chief Saif al-Adel has been captured or killed—including the network's Southeast Asia kingpin and the chief architect of the 9/11 attacks. And yet al-Qaeda's lethal ambitions, its capacity to reinvent itself and its pool of willing recruits remain inexhaustible. "Al-Qaeda isn't just surviving," says a top Pakistani intelligence officer. "From this region, it's planning new attacks all over the world, wherever it can strike." The Department of Homeland Security warned last week that al-Qaeda strategists are still aiming to pull off "synchronized attacks against U.S. interests"—including another attack on targets inside the U.S. involving commercial airliners hijacked in nearby countries. A senior federal law-enforcement official told TIME that U.S. intelligence believes multiple al-Qaeda operations are "already in the can" and that an attempted attack somewhere in the world is imminent.

Some counterterrorism experts believe

Figure 1.3 Photograph in an article. A photograph stands out from the surrounding body text, drawing the reader's attention and emphasizing a key point. (*Source: Time*, September 15, 2003, p. 60)

Illustrations should clarify and emphasize specific ideas in the text. They should be consistent with the ideas and information in your document and with your overall purpose as a writer.

1c Placing Elements

The placement of elements on a page helps readers understand the relationships among those elements. Placing elements next to or near each other suggests they are related (see Figure 1.4). Tables, charts, and graphs should be near the passages that cite them, making the ideas or information they are illustrating easier for readers to follow. Similarly, photographs and other images should be placed so their connection to particular passages is obvious.

Learn about illustrations on p. 77 and headers and footers on p. 48.

Figure 1.4 Illustration in a newsletter. The placement of this illustration shows its connection to the surrounding text.
(*Source: Comment Newsletter,* Colorado State University, September 5, 2002)

New building, walkway grace campus

Colorado State students enrolled in the sciences arrived on campus this fall in time to inaugurate the recently completed, $20 million Chemistry/Biosciences Hall. The 77,595-square-foot, five-story building houses a 250-seat lecture hall, 13 chemistry labs, nine biology labs and four biochemistry labs.

Centre Avenue, which runs under the building, is open to pedestrians, and other work is nearing completion, including installation of irrigation and landscaping, said Greg Smith, project manager for Facilities Management. A sculpture, part of the Art in Public Places project through the Colorado Council on the Arts, also will be installed on the north end of the avenue. All construction on Centre Avenue should be done by the end of September, Smith said.

The east side of Centre Avenue between Prospect Road and Lake Street has been changed to a no-parking zone, and a bike lane has been established, said Fred Haberecht, landscape architect for Facilities Management. A new section of the bikeway runs north along Centre Avenue to the Chemistry/Biosciences Hall, turns west between the Molecular and Radiological Biosciences Building and Chemistry Building and joins the existing bikeway at the intersection of Braiden Drive and Pitkin Street.

With this new work, a designated bike lane now runs through the center of campus from Prospect Street on the south to Laurel Street on the north.

New bike racks are available south of the new Chemistry/Biosciences Hall and east of the Chemistry Building.

The sculpture to be installed on the north side of Centre Avenue, called *Newton's Corner,* is a work by artist Howard Meehan from Santa Fe, N.M. See Page 8 for details on other new sculptures on campus. ■
– *Article and photo by Paul Miller*

1d Repeating Elements

Repeated elements, such as logos (like the Nike swoosh) or navigation menus on a Web site, help you achieve a unified design, a sense of identity, for your document (see Figure 1.5). Although this is particularly important for large, complex documents, such as Web sites and books, its importance should not be underestimated in smaller documents, such as essays and short articles. As readers move from page to page in a document, they usually expect navigation elements such as page numbers, headers and footers,

Learn about the elements of page layout on p. 43 and navigation aids on p. 60.

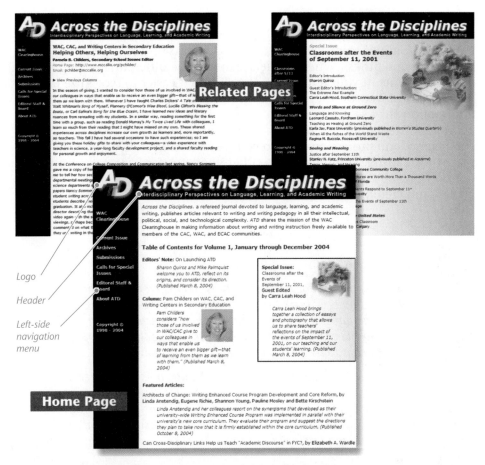

Logo

Header

Left-side
navigation
menu

Figure 1.5 Repeated elements on a Web site. Repeated use of a left-side menu, header, and logo helps establish a unified design for this Web site. Note the consistent use of fonts and colors that also contributes to the site's unified design. (*Source:* Colorado State University, *Across the Disciplines: Interdisciplinary Perspectives on Language, Learning and Academic Writing*)

and menus to appear in the same place on each page. When readers notice that repeated elements are missing on some pages or have different locations on different pages, their confidence in the quality of the document can be diminished.

1e Formatting Elements Consistently

Formatting elements consistently means treating each design element—headings, body text, illustrations and their captions, footnotes, and so on—the same way throughout your document. Consider, for instance, how the consistent design of the headings on the Web pages displayed in Figure 1.5 (a dark red color and extra spacing before and after each heading) differentiates the headings from the other textual elements on the pages, such as the body text and links. When readers can clearly differentiate among the design elements in your document, they'll find it easier to recognize the different roles played by the text and illustrations and be able to locate the information they seek faster.

A consistent design can also convey a sense of competence and professionalism to your readers. Consistent formatting, combined with other good design decisions, can increase your readers' confidence in the quality and credibility of a document.

Learn about formatting text on p. 36.

Design Activity

Collect a group of documents, such as magazine articles, academic essays and reports, book chapters, Web sites that have at least five pages, brochures, flyers, and scholarly journal articles. In a word processing file or a notebook, create a table like the one in Figure 1.6 and use it to record your reactions to the following:

1. *Examine the page layouts used in the documents to determine what types of balance they used. Note differences in the way your eyes move around pages laid out in asymmetrical and symmetrical designs. Which designs did you find most appealing, effective, and interesting?*

	Balance	Emphasis	Placement	Repetition	Consistency
Web Site					
Magazine Article					
Newspaper Article					
Essay					
Book Chapter					
Brochure					
Flyer					
Journal Article					

Figure 1.6 Chart for analyzing design.

2. *Identify strategies used in the documents to emphasize ideas and information. Some of your documents, for example, might use illustrations to emphasize a point, while others use text formatting. Ask yourself which strategies were most effective and least effective. Which strategies could have been used but were not?*

3. *Note differences in the ways writers have placed elements on their pages. Write down your reflections about the impact those placements had on your understanding of the documents.*

4. *Identify repeating elements in your collection of documents. Then identify elements that should have been repeated, such as menus or footers, but were not.*

5. *Examine your documents for evidence of consistent—or inconsistent—formatting of text and other elements on the pages. Think about your reactions to inconsistencies. Did the lack of consistency call your attention to the elements? If so, was that a good thing—that is, did it help emphasize a point?*

CHAPTER 2

Designing for a Purpose

A well-designed document frames ideas and information in a manner that helps you accomplish your purposes. Are you attempting to inform your readers? To provide an analysis of a complex issue? To persuade them to take action? Depending on your purposes, you might make design decisions that set a tone for your document, help your readers understand your points, convince your readers to accept an argument, and clarify or simplify the presentation of a complex concept.

2a Setting a Tone

One of the most powerful tools writers have for accomplishing their purpose is establishing an emotional context for readers. A document's tone is essentially an emotional appeal to its readers. Consider the tone adopted by Stanford University's Web site, The Martin Luther King, Jr. Papers Project (Figure 2.1). By adopting a serious, straightforward tone, the site conveys a sense of responsibility and competence. The balanced design of its opening page and its attractive use of illustrations and well-formatted text tell the reader that the site provides legitimate and unbiased information about its subject.

As the King site illustrates, the design principles of balance, emphasis, and consistency are particularly useful for setting a tone in your document. Unbalanced, or asymmetrical, designs tend to evoke a sense of motion, while balanced, or symmetrical, designs—often used in formal documents such as business and legal writings—suggest a sense of rest and stability. You can set a tone by using a particular color scheme, such as bright, cheerful hues, or by selecting photographs or drawings with a strong emotional impact. Consider, for example, your emotional response to the two-page introduction to *Time* magazine's September 2003 retrospective on the September 11 attacks, shown in Figure 2.2. The gritty, gray tones and text evoke

Figure 2.1 The Martin Luther King, Jr. Papers Project Web site. This site has balance, emphasis, and consistent text formatting, which give it a serious, straightforward tone. (*Source:* The Martin Luther King, Jr. Papers Project, Stanford University. http://www.stanford.edu/group/King)

Figure 2.2 *Time* magazine article. The opening pages of a retrospective on the 9/11 attacks use images and a gray color scheme to set a mood for readers. (*Source: Time,* September 15, 2003, pp. 32–33)

a somber mood, while the images themselves—fire-fighters working in the shadow of a shattered building—bring to mind the sacrifice and dedication of the rescue workers who labored in the wake of the tragedy.

Learn about using color on p. 66 and using illustrations on p. 77.

2b Helping Readers Understand a Point

The design principles of emphasis and placement are particularly useful for introducing and helping readers understand your points—main or otherwise. Formatting specific textual elements, such as headings or pull quotes, allows you to call your readers' attention to important ideas and information. To introduce a main point, you might use a bold font, a typeface different from the one used in the rest of the document, or a different color to signal the importance of information contained in a pull quote, subheading, or caption (see Figure 2.3).

Learn about using fonts on p. 35.

You can use these principles to stress key points in a document. For example, you can highlight a definition or example by formatting text in a contrasting font or color, adding borders to the passage, or placing text in a pull quote. You can also use illustrations such as photographs, drawings,

Figure 2.3 Article that conveys a main point. Text pulled into the margin in a larger font and contrasting color—sometimes referred to as a marginal gloss—as well as a photograph set at an unusual angle with a caption help readers understand the main point of this article.

(*Source: Sunset,* July 2003, p. 148)

Horse haven

Even in grainy color, he is every inch the celebrity—coddled, glistening, surrounded by his retinue.

"It was uncertain times," Tracy Livingston says. "People were looking for a hero." He is talking about the star of this particular home movie, Seabiscuit—one of the United States' most famous racehorses—filmed in the late '30s as he arrived at Northern California's Ridgewood Ranch.

We must still be looking for heroes, because 63 years after his last racetrack triumph, the United States is in the

Ridgewood Ranch is a key part of the Seabiscuit saga

middle of a second Seabiscuit boom. *Seabiscuit: An American Legend,* Laura Hillenbrand's equine biography, is cantering across the best-seller lists. This month, the horse goes Hollywood in *Seabiscuit,* a film starring Jeff Bridges and Tobey Maguire.

Ridgewood Ranch is an essential part of the Seabiscuit saga. The ranch near Willits, California, was the dream of Charles Howard, who parlayed a San Francisco Buick dealership into a life among the landed gentry. He bought Ridgewood in 1921. Later, encouraged by his horse-loving wife, he began to invest in horse racing and, in 1936, spent $8,000 on a 3-year-old bay named Seabiscuit. The stubby horse didn't look promising. But with

triumph, Seabiscuit ruptured a leg. Pollard, meanwhile, lay in after a bone-shattering racetra whispered, would ever race a both to Ridgewood to recover

It's a good place to recove now. With its rolling hills risi

Seabiscuit's legacy lives on, thanks in part to Tracy Livingston.

That is what Livingston an With help from the Willits

✉ **E-mail This Page**

Norman Lear: Empowering the Youth Vote
Producer Launches Campaign to Encourage Young Voters

🔊 Morning Edition audio

Nov. 13, 2003 -- Norman Lear, one of Hollywood's leading television and film producers, is launching a drive to encourage young people to vote in next year's election. The *All in the Family* creator -- who bought an original copy of the Declaration of Independence and sent it on a multi-year nationwide tour -- discusses the new voter initiative with NPR's Renee Montagne.

Voter turnout among 18- to 24-year-olds is generally far lower than the overall voting population. In 2000, about 36 percent of the young group reported that it voted, compared to nearly 60 percent for all voters, according to the Census Bureau.

In July 2001, Norman Lear announces the kick-off of a three-and-a-half year cross-country tour of the Declaration of Independence.
Credit: The Declaration of Independence Road Trip

Lear cites studies that show the importance of getting young adults to vote as soon as they turn 18. "If you get that person to vote, inspire that person to vote the first time, the chances are much greater that they will vote for the rest of their lives," he says.

» Youth Voting Trends

"If you... inspire that [young] person to vote the first time, the chances are much greater that they will vote for the rest of their lives."

Norman Lear

One of the reasons young people cite for not voting is that they "don't feel sufficiently informed," Lear says. "One of the things we want to do is encourage young people to know that they are far more informed than they think they are. And, more important than that, once

MORNING EDITION®
with Bob Edwards

latest show

previous shows

radio expeditions

talking plants

about morning edition

where can i hear it?

morning@npr.org

Figure 2.4
National Public Radio Web site. This design uses a photograph, a caption, and a pull quote formatted to contrast with the body text to help readers focus on the key points.
(*Source:* National Public Radio, http://npr.org)

charts, graphs, or tables. Note, for instance, how the text pulled out of the main body of the text in Figure 2.4 calls readers' attention to the key point of the article, while the photograph and its caption supply additional information.

Learn about using marginal glosses and pull quotes on p. 54.

2c Convincing Readers to Accept a Point

The key to convincing readers is providing them with appropriate, relevant evidence. You can help your readers accept an argument by using design elements, including illustrations, marginal glosses, pull quotes, and bulleted lists, to call attention to that evidence. The striking photograph in Figure 2.5, for example, evokes an emotional response by linking cigarettes with death and smoking-related health issues, and draws the reader's attention not only to the image but to the text. The list not only has bullets—an eye-catching technique—but boldface text as well.

Learn about using bulleted lists on p. 53.

Figure 2.5 American Lung Association of Texas Web site. This design uses a photograph, a bulleted list, and bold text to highlight key reasons why smokers should quit. (*Source:* American Lung Association. Copyright American Lung Association of Texas Web site, http://www.texaslung.org)

Why You Should Quit

Smoking-related diseases kill more than 440,000 Americans every year. More than 26,000 of those lives are lost right here in Texas.

Smoking causes 87% of all lung cancer cases and most cases of emphysema and chronic bronchitis.

If you've tried quitting, you're not alone. Cigarette smoking can be a hard habit to break because:

- **Nicotine is physically addicting.** You actually feel a craving for cigarettes.

- **The force of habit is strong.** Smoking may seem a necessary part of your daily life.

2d Clarifying Complex Concepts

Sometimes a picture really is worth a thousand words. Instead of trying to explain a complex concept with words alone, add an illustration. A well-chosen, well-placed photograph, flow chart, diagram, or table can clarify a detailed topic—photosynthesis, for example—in less space and, in many cases, more effectively than a long text passage (see Figure 2.6).

Bulleted and numbered lists can also help clarify the key elements of a complex concept. Bulleted and numbered lists use the design principle of emphasis to call attention to the most important aspects of a complex concept. Typically, bulleted and numbered lists

Learn about using illustrations on p. 77.

are set off from the main text with additional space in the left margin. Boldface, italics, and underlines can be used in the list to further emphasize the most important information.

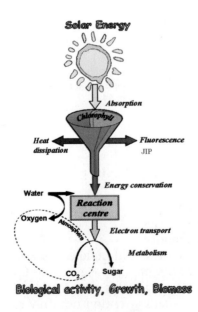

Figure 2.6 Diagram that clarifies a complex concept. (*Source:* APTE Association)

Design Activity

Collect a set of documents, such as essays, articles, Web sites, brochures, and flyers, that are written to inform or persuade readers. In a word processing file or a notebook, create a table like the one in Figure 2.7 and use it to record your reactions to the following:

1. *Note how each document made you feel when you first saw it, and identify how color schemes, images, and page designs help set the tone.*

2. *Examine how the design principles of emphasis and placement are used to introduce and help readers understand key points in your documents. Pay particular attention to the font formatting, color, shading, borders, and illustrations. Record the key strategies used in each document to highlight important ideas and information.*

3. *Review your documents for examples of the use of design to make points more convincing for readers. Identify which design strategies were used for this purpose, and jot down your thoughts about their effectiveness and appropriateness.*

4. *Scan your documents for lists and illustrations. Determine whether these techniques help clarify complex concepts. If so, evaluate their effectiveness at conveying complex information to readers, and write down your evaluation in your table.*

	Tone	Understanding	Convincing	Clarifying
Essay				
Magazine Article				
Newspaper Article				
Web Site				
Brochure				
Flyer				
Journal Article				

Figure 2.7 Chart for analyzing design.

CHAPTER 3

Designing for Your Readers

A well-designed document helps readers locate the information they are seeking quickly and with a minimum of effort. It is also easy on your readers' eyes: They don't have to strain to read the text or discern illustrations. Text, images, and other features of the document work together to help readers move through the document. Document design can improve the organization of your document, make certain information easier to locate, and help readers recognize the function of different parts of your document. Paying attention to the practical aspects of how a document works for your readers will result in a more appealing, persuasive, and easy-to-read document.

3a Helping Readers Understand the Organization of a Document

Even relatively brief documents, such as brochures and newspaper articles, can contain a considerable amount of information. Headings and subheadings can be helpful because they signal the content of sections in the document. As you design your headings and subheadings, keep in mind the design principles of emphasis, repetition, and consistency. Format your headings so that they stand out from other parts of the document—like the headings and subheadings in this book do—and format each of them consistently (see Figure 3.1). This will help your readers progress more easily through your document.

Learn about using headings and subheadings on p. 48.

3b Helping Readers Locate Information and Ideas

Many longer print documents use tables of contents and indexes to help readers locate information and ideas. Web sites, especially those with more than 20 pages, typically provide a mix of menus and navigation headers and

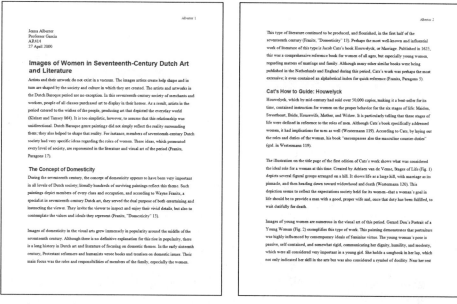

Figure 3.1 Use of headings in an academic essay. Headings and subheadings, set off from the main body text in a contrasting font and color, help readers understand the organization of a document.

footers to help readers move around the site. Some complex sites also provide tables of contents and graphical site indexes (a graphical representation of key pages on a Web site) to help readers locate information. When these navigation aids are integrated into pages, they are often distinguished from the surrounding text with bordered or shaded boxes or with fonts that differ from those used in the main body of the document (see Figure 3.2).

Learn about using navigation aids on p. 60.

institutions and the dates of the campus lectures will be posted on the ΦBK website in early fall.

Hill. Each host chapter provides a service fee to the national office and is responsible for all local expenses.

In This Issue

Rye Schwartz-Barcott, trying a dance step with] munity organization there called Carolina For]

Figure 3.2 Magazine table of contents. A table of contents, titled "In This Issue," at the beginning of a magazine helps readers locate information.

(*Source:* Phi Beta Kappa *Key Reporter,* Spring 2003)

3c Helping Readers Recognize the Function of Parts of a Document

In a well-designed document, your decisions about design will most often be made for functional, as opposed to decorative, reasons. For example, headers and footers serve a particular function on a page: They tell readers where they are in the document by supplying the page numbers, the title of the document, or a section heading. Headers and footers are positioned and formatted so they are clearly distinguished from the main text.

Learn about using color on p. 66, and shading, borders, and rules on p. 72.

Signaling the function of specific parts of a document has become increasingly important in assignments for writing classes. As students have begun to write more complex documents, such as articles and Web sites, they are using strategies commonly found in print and online publications. Sidebars and "For More Information" sections, for example, are showing up with greater frequency in academic documents. To help readers recognize that these parts of the document differ from the main text, they can be designed to stand out. Using the design principle of emphasis, for example, you might format a sidebar in an article with a shaded or colored box so the reader knows that the information in the sidebar is separate from the main body (see Figure 3.3). Similarly, you might format a list of related readings or Web links differently on a Web page so its function is clear to the reader.

If you use elements such as headers, footers, and sidebars, design them consistently. By formatting sidebars in a particular way, you can distinguish them from "For More Information" boxes, pull quotes, and other design elements. Signaling these functions visually allows readers to decide quickly whether they want to divert their attention from the body of the document.

Figure 3.3 Sidebar in an article. This sidebar is formatted with a colored box to stand out from the body text. (*Source: PC World,* June 2003, p. 52)

Design Activity

Select one or more documents that use headings and subheadings; navigation tools such as menus or tables of contents; and text with different types of functions, such as headers, footers, or sidebars. If you have difficulty finding a document, consider using this book. Then respond to the following:

1. *Examine the use of headings and subheadings in the document you've chosen. Keeping in mind the use of headings and subheadings to help readers understand the organization of a document, give it a grade. Write a brief justification of your grade.*

2. *List the types of navigation tools, such as menus on a Web site, page numbers in print documents, headers and footers, tables of contents, and indexes, used in the document you've chosen. For each entry in your list, consider its effectiveness and appropriateness for helping readers find their way through the document. Next to each entry in the list, provide a grade and a justification for that grade.*

3. *Identify different types of text used in your document. For example, you might note that the document contains body text, block quotations, a header or footer, page numbers, or sidebars. Ask yourself whether you could quickly recognize the function of a particular type of text. For example, could you tell the difference between body text and a sidebar, or between body text and a header? Give the document a grade for its use of color, text formatting, and other design elements to distinguish the functions of the different types of text used in the document. Briefly justify your grade.*

CHAPTER 4

Designing for Medium and Genre

Writers of well-designed documents recognize the opportunities and limitations associated with reading documents published in a particular medium, such as high-quality print, newsprint, or one of the many digital formats. For example, flyers and brochures are often printed in color, although the expense of producing large quantities of color flyers and brochures can cause the documents to be printed in black and white. In contrast, digital documents such as word processing files and Web pages can be easily distributed via electronic mail or by sharing a Web address (URL) with potential readers.

Writers should also recognize that readers bring particular expectations to different types of documents, or **genres**, such as essays, books, or Web sites. Readers won't expect to find a great deal of information in a flyer, for instance. However, they will expect an academic essay to contain well-developed ideas and supporting evidence.

As you consider the design of your document, reflect on how you can adapt to publication medium and genre, as well as to related issues such as page size and screen resolution.

4a Adapting to Your Publication Medium

Well-designed documents take advantage of the characteristics of print or digital media. If you are printing your document, focus your attention on design choices that are appropriate for print documents, such as the use of color, headings and subheadings, and sidebars. Consider whether you have the resources available to create a document that makes extensive use of color. If you are producing a single document, as would be the case for most academic assignments, you might need only a color printer. If you are planning to make a lot of copies at a copy center or commercial printer, however, compare the cost of color versus black and white. In addition, consider related issues such as the quality, cost, and dimensions of the paper you want to use.

If you are designing a digital document, such as a Web site, an e-mail newsletter, or a word processing document, focus on other issues, such as the impact of screen size and resolution on the ease with which text can be read, the expanded range of illustrations that can be integrated into a document, and the speed with which an image can be downloaded from the Web.

4b Adapting to Genre Constraints

Readers familiar with particular genres of documents, such as newspaper columns, informative brochures, and feature articles, expect documents in a genre to share a particular look and feel. Newspaper articles, for example, are typically laid out in narrow columns of text and are often accompanied by captioned photographs. Informative Web sites typically include links and a page containing contact information. The design of specific genres reflects the decisions groups of writers and readers have made over time about such issues as the purpose, style, and types of evidence used in a document. Understanding the design choices typically associated with a particular genre, as a result, involves understanding the reasons behind those decisions. As you design your document, consider not only the typical design characteristics associated with the genre you've chosen, but also the reasons underlying those decisions. You can read more about the choices associated with genres typically assigned in writing and writing-intensive courses in Part Three: Designing Documents.

Learn about the types of illustrations that can be used in digital documents on p. 77.

4c Considering Page Size and Screen Resolution

A key consideration in document design is the size of your page or, if you are working in a digital format, the resolution of the screen on which your document will be read. Depending on your genre, you might have little or no choice of page size or screen resolution. Essays assigned in writing courses, for example, are usually printed on letter-size paper. Readers of Web sites, rather than writers, control the size and resolution of the screens on which they view a site—although many Web developers design their sites for a specific resolution. For genres in which you can choose the page size or screen resolution, such as brochures, flyers, or multimedia presentations, consider how your choice can help you achieve your purposes and meet your readers' expectations.

Design Activity

Find one example of each type of document discussed in Part Three of this book. You could use one of your academic essays, an article from a newspaper or magazine, and virtually any Web site. You can easily find brochures in your college or community library and flyers on a bulletin board on campus. If you have difficulty finding a multimedia presentation, check out "The Nation's Report Card: U.S. History 2001" on the Web at http://nces.ed.gov/nationsreportcard/data/ppt/ushistorypress052002.ppt.

Create two lists:

1. *Design elements found in all five documents. Your list might include the use of margins and font formatting. It might also include color, borders, and shading.*

2. *Design elements that are found in only one or two of the documents.*

After you've created your lists, compare them. Write a brief analysis of why some design elements are common to all of the documents you collected and why others are not.

CHAPTER 5

Designing with Your Sources in Mind

A well-designed document identifies the sources of the information, ideas, and illustrations used within it. A well-designed document also uses illustrations appropriately—that is, it uses illustrations in a manner consistent with copyright law and fair use principles. Designing with your sources in mind begins, then, with determining whether it is appropriate to use a particular source in your document. Once you've determined that it's appropriate to use information from a source, consider how you will acknowledge that source. If you are writing a document in response to a course assignment or for submission to an academic or professional journal, you will most likely be expected to conform to the requirements of documentation systems, such as those created by the Modern Language Association (MLA) and American Psychological Association (APA). In most cases, you'll find that the documentation system provides guidelines for acknowledging sources and for labeling and formatting illustrations.

5a Avoiding Plagiarism: Considering Copyright and Fair Use

The Web has made it easier to locate a wide range of sources that provide information in textual, visual, and audio formats. Unfortunately, access to these sources has made it easier to plagiarize the work of others. Plagiarism, a form of intellectual dishonesty, involves unintentionally using someone else's work without properly acknowledging where the ideas came from (the most common form of plagiarism) or intentionally copying someone else's work and passing it off as your own (the most serious form of plagiarism).

Plagiarism is based on the notion of copyright, or ownership of a document or idea. Like a patent that protects an invention or a trademark that protects a name or symbol for a product, a copyright protects an author's investment of time and energy into the creation of a document. Essentially, it provides authors with an assurance that someone else can't steal their work and profit from it without penalty.

In most cases, plagiarism is unintentional. And most cases of unintentional plagiarism, it turns out, result from failing to keep track of or acknowledge sources, taking poor notes, or misunderstanding the rules of fair use. If you do any of the following, you are plagiarizing:

- Neglect to list the source of a paraphrase, quotation, or summary in your text or in your works cited or references list.
- Quote a passage in a note but neglect to include quotation marks. Later, you insert the quotation into your document without realizing it's a direct quotation.
- Attempt to paraphrase a passage but change only a few words. Your paraphrase differs so slightly from the original that it might as well be a direct quotation.
- Create a summary based on key sentences from several paragraphs in a source. Your summary becomes a series of paraphrases so similar to the original sentences that the summary is simply a selective copy of the source.
- Fail to distinguish between your ideas and ideas that come from your sources.

As you design your document, it's particularly important to consider the rules of copyright and fair use regarding the use of digital illustrations, such as photographs and other images, audio clips, video clips, and animations. The **fair use provision**, which is defined in Section 107 of the Copyright Act of 1976 (available at http://www.copyright.gov/title17/92chap1.html#107), allows you to use copyrighted materials for purposes of criticism, comment, news reporting, teaching, scholarship, or research, provided that you acknowledge the source of the material. You can usually use up to 10 percent of a source, although this amount can be substantially less for songs or poetry and substantially more for images and other forms of digital content.

If you intend to publish your document, you might need to request permission to use an image. An e-mail message or a phone call might be the quickest way to obtain permission. If contact information is not provided in the source from which you have taken the image, but you know the name of the author or publisher of the source, consider using the "people search" tools on Web search sites such as Yahoo! and Lycos. When requesting permission, give the author or publisher your name; the college, university, or company with which you are affiliated (if any); why you want to use the source; the document in which it will appear; and how widely that document will be distributed. If you talk on the phone, ask for written permission, either on paper or as an e-mail message. Don't forget to provide your own contact information so replies can be returned to you.

5b Helping Readers Locate Your Source Citations

If you are working on a document that will be distributed in print, you'll find that most genres have distinctive procedures for identifying the sources used in a document. For example, articles or essays published in scholarly or professional journals typically require the inclusion of a works cited list, reference list, or bibliography. Articles written for newspapers and magazines usually require that the source of information, ideas, or illustrations be identified within the text of the document or in a caption accompanying an illustration. In addition, a number of print genres, such as essays written for class assignments, allow the use of endnotes and footnotes, as well as marginal notes, to help readers locate sources. If you are working with a digital document, such as a Web site, you can use not only the techniques available in print documents, but also pop-up windows that link to a page containing information about the source, links to a bibliography, or links to the source itself, assuming it is available online (see Figure 5.1).

Figure 5.1 Pop-up window with works cited list. A pop-up window (**A**) containing a works cited list opens when a link in the main body of a Web page (**B**) is clicked.

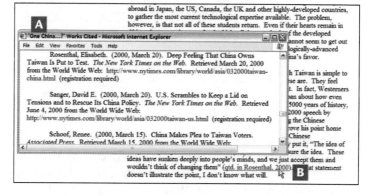

5c Considering the Design Guidelines of Documentation Systems

The major documentation systems typically used in writing or writing-intensive courses—such as those found in the *Chicago Manual of Style* and in guides published by the Modern Language Association (MLA), the American Psychological Association (APA), and the Council of Science Editors (CSE)—provide guidelines that can affect the design of your document. If you are working on a writing project in which you must conform to the standards of a particular documentation system, consult its guidelines for advice on the format of works cited lists, the placement and labeling of illustrations, and the format of cover pages.

Figure 5.2
MLA guide-
lines for
formatting
illustrations.

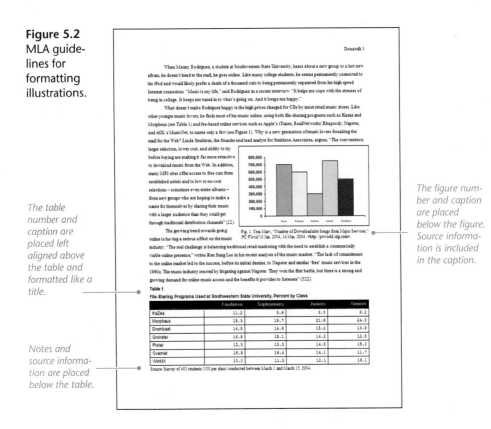

The table number and caption are placed left aligned above the table and formatted like a title.

The figure number and caption are placed below the figure. Source information is included in the caption.

Notes and source information are placed below the table.

If you are working on an assignment for a course, consult your instructor about how to handle the advice provided by the documentation system you are following. In general, you'll find that the guidelines for most documentation systems assume that you are creating a manuscript that will be formatted for publication at a later date. As a result, they tend to recommend that you double-space the lines in your document, use wide margins, and avoid the use of formatting in headings and subheadings, practices that work well for academic essays but are seldom appropriate for published articles and Web sites. The leading documentation systems also provide guidance about issues such as the location of headers and footers, appropriate formatting of page numbers, and the use of title pages.

The documentation systems also provide guidelines for working with illustrations, such as photographs, drawings, video and audio clips, animations, charts, graphs, and tables. Once again, these guidelines reflect an assumption that your document will be formatted for publication at a later date. In general, the documentation systems recommend that you should do the following:

- Place an illustration as close as possible to the parts of the text to which it relates.
- Distinguish between tables and figures.
- Number tables and figures in the order in which they appear in the document.
- Use compound numbering of figures and tables in longer documents. For example, the second table in Chapter 5 would be labeled Table 5.2.

The documentation systems differ, however, in their advice about the placement of labels, captions, notes, and source material in tables and figures (see Figure 5.2), so be sure to consult the particular documentation system that you are using for specific guidelines on how to handle this material. Remember that, although these guidelines vary, they share the goal of using illustrations consistently and presenting them as effectively as possible.

Design Activity

Find three documents that use information from sources. The documents should be of different types. You might choose among academic essays, scholarly books, magazine or newspaper articles, scholarly articles, Web sites, multimedia presentations, and brochures. Write down responses to the following:

1. *Examine each document to determine how it acknowledges sources within the text. Ask yourself, for example, whether it uses a parenthetical documentation system, such as the MLA or APA systems, which lists only the name of the author and a page number or year of publication of the source.*

2. *Determine whether each document uses a works cited or reference list.*

3. *Keeping in mind the likely readers of the documents you've chosen, write a brief analysis of the appropriateness and effectiveness of the techniques used in the three documents to identify sources.*

PART TWO

Understanding Design Elements

Document design was once considered an afterthought in the composing process—something done to a document only after planning, drafting, reviewing, revising, and editing had been completed. Technological limitations in twentieth-century publishing made it difficult—and in some cases impossible—for writers to play a role in the design of documents. That work was left to editors and designers, specialists who worked with completed manuscripts after writers had turned them over. As a result, writers gave little thought to how design might enhance their documents.

Today, technology has given writers far greater control over the design of their documents. Consider these technological advances:

- Word processing programs allow writers to create elegant page layouts; develop sophisticated charts, graphs, and tables; use a wide range of illustrations (including multimedia); and work effectively with fonts and colors.
- Color printers enable writers to publish attractive documents at a fraction of the cost once required for complex color documents.
- New versions of word processing programs, such as Microsoft Word and Corel WordPerfect, offer design tools that surpass the most sophisticated desktop publishing programs of past decades as well as tools that allow writers to create attractive and effective Web sites.

Writers, in effect, have become designers. Design is no longer something applied only after the document has been written. Instead, it is considered throughout the composing process. Writers might decide to use headings and subheadings, for example, before they've written a single sentence. Using headings and subheadings not only simplifies the process of creating transitions and makes it easier for readers to understand the overall organization of information and ideas in the document, but it also helps writers plan and organize their documents. Writers might also create flowcharts or diagrams rather than writing lengthy passages describing complex processes. And, rather than allowing editors to search for an appropriate photograph to set the mood for an essay, writers might find and insert photographs themselves.

Your efforts to design effective documents will be shaped by your understanding of several key design elements. Part Two introduces you to the roles of fonts, line spacing, and alignment; page layout, navigation aids, and color; shading, borders, and rules; and illustrations—all key elements of document design.

CHAPTER 6

Fonts, Line Spacing, and Alignment

Making decisions about fonts, line spacing, and alignment is the writer's most common creative process when it comes to design. It is also among the most important, because poor choices can make a document difficult to read.

6a Fonts

Fonts are a complete set of type of a particular size and face—for example, 12-point Times New Roman or 10-point Helvetica. To learn how to choose appropriate fonts, you must first understand some basic font terminology.

Typeface   The design of a particular font, such as Arial, Garamond, or Times New Roman.

Style   The format of the font. In addition to regular body text, you may choose to apply *italics,* **bold,** or ***bold italics*** to your text.

Family   A set of fonts that is a variation on a basic typeface. The Arial family, for example, includes *Arial Italic,* **Arial Bold,** ***Arial Bold Italic***, Arial Narrow, **Arial Rounded Bold,** and **Arial Black**.

Effects   Changes made to a particular font, such as underlining or superscripting. Common effects include the following:

<u>Underline</u>	ALL CAPS	Superscript ^{12}
~~Strike Through~~	SMALL CAPS	Subscript $_{12}$

Size   Font size is measured in **points**, with 72 points to an inch. Typically, body text is 10 to 12 points, and heading type is 14 points or larger. In general, a body text size of 10 to 12 points is the easiest to read in print and Web documents.

Fixed-Width and Variable-Width Fonts   Fixed-width fonts, such as Courier and other "typewriter" fonts, are set so that the space given to each letter, number, and symbol has the same width. In fixed-width fonts, therefore, the letter l and the letter w take up the same width. In contrast, the width of letters, numbers, and symbols in variable-width fonts, such as Helvetica and Times New Roman, is based on their natural width. In general, variable-width fonts are easier to read. Fixed-width fonts are useful, however, when you need to align text in columns, such as you might do with a budget or a set of descriptive statistics, such as populations of states or countries (see Figure 6.1).

COUNTY	POPULATION
St. Louis	199,983
Hennepin	1,122,259
Ramsey	510,568
Itasca	44,144

Figure 6.1   Using a fixed-width font for numbers.

Categories of Fonts   The two main categories of fonts are serif and sans serif. **Serif fonts**, such as Times New Roman, have small brush strokes or lines at the end of each stroke. Serif fonts are considered more readable for longer passages of text and thus are often used for body text. **Sans serif fonts**, such as Arial and Helvetica, do not have serifs. Many writers use sans serif fonts for headings and subheadings. Additional font categories include **dec-**

How to Format Fonts

To format fonts in Microsoft Word, use one of the following techniques:

Menu Commands   Choose the `Format > Font` command from the main menu. You can also select the `Font` command with your mouse by right clicking (Windows) or control clicking (Macintosh).

Toolbar Buttons   You can use the toolbar to format fonts by clicking on icons in the formatting toolbar. If all of these icons do not appear on your toolbar, you can add them using the `Tools > Customize` command from the main menu.

Keyboard Commands   The most common keyboard commands in Windows are `CTRL-b` (bold), `CTRL-i` (italics), and `CTRL-u` (underline). To use these commands, hold down the Control key (`CTRL`) while you press the b, i, or u key. On the Macintosh, use the Command key (⌘).

MENU

TOOLBAR

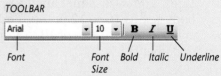

Font   Font   Bold   Italic   Underline
            Size

orative fonts and **symbol fonts.** The following are examples of all four categories:

ABCDEF Serif fonts: Times, Times New Roman, Garamond, Century Schoolbook, Bookman Old Style, Goudy Old Style

ABCDEF Sans serif fonts: Helvetica, Arial, Universe, Verdana, Gill Sans, Tahoma, Zurich Light

ABCDEF Decorative fonts: Algerian, Bernhard Fashion, Brush Script, Monotype Corsiva, Keypunch

✛✚✢✣✦✳ Symbol fonts: Wingdings, Common Bullets, Zapf Dingbats

6b Font Guidelines

To increase the readability of your document, keep the following guidelines in mind:

1. Select fonts that are easy to read. The reason certain fonts are used as the default in word processors, such as Microsoft Word, is that they are typically easy to read. Times New Roman, for instance, is much easier to read than **KEYPUNCH**.

Consider as well the medium in which your readers will read your document. On paper, serif fonts, such as Garamond and Times New Roman, are generally easier to read. Some research suggests, however, that sans serif fonts may be easier to read on the screen. Verdana, for instance, is a sans serif font that was developed specifically for reading on a computer monitor.

Finally, remember that variable-width fonts make it easier to read body text, while fixed-width fonts, such as Courier or Lucida Sans Typewriter, make it easier to read a column of numbers.

2. Select fonts that complement each other. A serif body font, such as Times New Roman, Century Schoolbook, or Garamond, works well with a sans serif heading font, such as Arial, Helvetica, Lucida Sans, or Verdana. If you prefer to use a sans serif font for body text, consider using a serif font for headings.

3. Avoid using too many fonts, styles, and effects. Figures 6.2 and 6.3 show the same Web page designed with appropriate and inappropriate use of fonts. Don't go overboard with fonts. Generally, use no more than four different fonts in a document. For example, you can use one for your body text, another for your headings, another for long quotations, and another for fixed-width needs, such as text in tables. Choosing fonts at random or because they are "interesting" can have disastrous effects, such as making a document difficult to read or confusing readers about the purpose or

The writer used multiple fonts, styles, and effects, creating a confused look.

A combination of serif and sans serif fonts, italics, and bold text creates a distracting passage of text.

Figure 6.2 Web site that uses fonts inappropriately.

The writer used a sans serif font for links in the menu. All are the same size and face.

The writer used a serif font for body text.

Figure 6.3 Web site that uses fonts appropriately.

function of particular passages. Similarly, extensive use of *italics,* **bold,** underline, SMALL CAPS, or any of the other styles and effects makes it harder to read a document. Use styles and effects for their intended purpose only: to emphasize your points and to signal the function of particular parts of your text, such as long quotations or superscripted footnotes.

4. **Exercise caution when using fonts in digital documents.** Word processing and desktop publishing programs provide a great deal of control over fonts. If you are planning to distribute your documents in digital format, however, be aware that the fonts you use seldom travel with your document. (Some programs allow you to embed fonts when you save a file.) Web pages suffer from the same limitation. If the readers of your Web site do not have a certain font on their computer, their Web browsers will use a substitute font. The resulting page, as viewed through their browsers, could have an appearance that differs markedly from what you intended.

6c   Line Spacing

Line spacing refers to the amount of space between lines of text. It is also referred to as leading—the term for the thickness of the lead spacers that used to be placed between lines of text when type was set by hand. In most word processing and desktop publishing programs, you can specify the space between lines of text as well as before and after paragraphs and headings. Spacing can be set precisely, using points (there are 72 points per vertical inch of text), or it can be set relatively, using lines (single-spacing, double-spacing, triple-spacing, and so on). Consider the difference between the following blocks of text that have different line spacing.

This is 10-point Garamond with 8 points of line spacing. Notice how the descenders (the bottoms of letters such as g, p, and y) and the ascenders (tops of letters such as d, h, and l) collide.

This is 10-point Garamond with 12 points of line spacing.

This is 10-point Garamond with 15 points of line spacing.

To ensure that text is easy to read, line spacing should be at least one or two points greater than the height of the text itself. For example, 10-point text should be set with at least 11 or 12 points of line spacing. When text is crammed together vertically, it is both difficult to read and hard to insert written comments. Keep this in mind if you are creating a document such as an essay on which a teacher or supervisor might write comments.

How to Format Alignment and Spacing

You can format alignment and spacing in Microsoft Word by selecting the text you want to format and then using one of the following techniques:

MENU

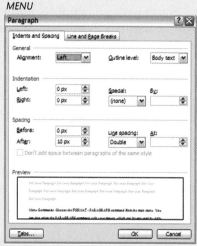

Menu Commands Choose the `Format >` `Paragraph` command from the main menu. You can also select the `Paragraph` command with your mouse by right clicking (Windows) or control clicking (Macintosh).

Toolbar Buttons You can use the toolbar to format alignment and spacing by clicking on icons in the Formatting toolbar. If all of these icons do not appear on your toolbar, you can add them using the `Tools > Customize` command from the main menu.

Keyboard Commands You can use the following keyboard commands in Windows by selecting the text you want to format and holding down the Control key (`CTRL`) while you use the following

TOOLBAR ALIGNMENT   *LINE SPACING*

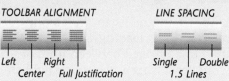

Left   Right   Single   Double
   Center   Full Justification   1.5 Lines

Control key combinations: `CTRL-l` for left justified, `CTRL-r` for right justified, `CTRL-e` for centered, `CTRL-j` for full justified, `CTRL-1` for single line spacing, `CTRL-5` for 1.5 line spacing, and `CTRL-2` for double line spacing. On the Macintosh, use the Command key (⌘).

6d Alignment

Alignment refers to the placement of text and illustrations (such as photos and drawings) on the page. You can select four types of alignment: left, right, centered, and justified (see Figure 6.4).

Left aligned (ragged right) text is typically the easiest to read. In contrast, justified text offers an attractive, finished look to a document, and it can be particularly effective in documents that contain columns. Be aware, however, that justified text can slow down the reader because it can produce irregular spacing between words. In addition, it can result in an excess of hyphenated words, which can also make the reading process slower. Finally, because word processing software does not always hyphenate words properly, readers may find themselves slowing down as they puzzle over hyphens in unexpected places.

Figure 6.4 Left, right, centered, and justified alignment of text.

One of the greatest monsters to slay before an applicant can enter through college doors is that of the standardized testing used by colleges to assess capability. Many colleges use the traditional forms of testing such as the SAT's, ACT's and other college entrance exams as a standard procedure in evaluating academic capability. In the book "Getting In," Levine and May state that, "A college entrance examination is one of the two most significant factors in getting into college, the other being high school grades" (Levine and May 116).

Left aligned: The lines of text and illustrations are aligned flush to the left margin and "ragged" (unaligned) to the right margin.

One of the greatest monsters to slay before an applicant can enter through college doors is that of the standardized testing used by colleges to assess capability. Many colleges use the traditional forms of testing such as the SAT's, ACT's and other college entrance exams as a standard procedure in evaluating academic capability. In the book "Getting In," Levine and May state that, "A college entrance examination is one of the two most significant factors in getting into college, the other being high school grades" (Levine and May 116).

Right aligned: The lines of text and illustrations are aligned flush to the right margin and "ragged" (unaligned) to the left margin.

One of the greatest monsters to slay before an applicant can enter through college doors is that of the standardized testing used by colleges to assess capability. Many colleges use the traditional forms of testing such as the SAT's, ACT's and other college entrance exams as a standard procedure in evaluating academic capability. In the book "Getting In," Levine and May state that, "A college entrance examination is one of the two most significant factors in getting into college, the other being high school grades" (Levine and May 116).

Centered: Lines of text and illustrations are centered horizontally on the page.

One of the greatest monsters to slay before an applicant can enter through college doors is that of the standardized testing used by colleges to assess capability. Many colleges use the traditional forms of testing such as the SAT's, ACT's and other college entrance exams as a standard procedure in eval-uating academic capability. In the book "Getting In," Levine and May state that, "A college entrance examination is one of the two most significant factors in getting into col-lege, the other being high school grades" (Levine and May 116).

Justified: Lines of text and illustrations are aligned to both the right and left margins, usually by inserting extra spacing between words within the line.

Design Activity

Reformatting an existing document can help you understand how design elements can affect effectiveness and usability. To explore the impact of font formatting, line spacing, and alignment on effectiveness and usability, reformat a copy of an academic essay you've written for a class by doing the following:

- *Change the body font used in the document. Apply different serif and sans serif typefaces, and experiment with styles such as bold and italics.*

- *If the document uses headings and subheadings, apply different typefaces, styles, effects, and sizes to them.*

- *Change the line spacing in the document.*

- *Experiment with left aligned, right aligned, centered, and fully justified text.*

Write a brief summary of what you have learned about these elements of design by reformatting your essay.

CHAPTER 7

Page Layout

Page layout involves the placement of text, illustrations, and other objects on a page or screen. Successful page layout draws on a number of design elements, including page grids, white space, margins and gutters, columns, headers and footers, page numbers, headings and subheadings, bulleted and numbered lists, captions and bylines, marginal glosses and pull quotes, sidebars, and decorative elements such as drop caps. Most word processing programs set defaults for standard elements, but making conscious decisions about them allows you to control the display of text, illustrations, and other objects on the page or screen.

7a Page Grids

A page grid defines the standard placement of text and illustrations on the pages of your document. Page grids help you ensure a consistent design on all pages. In a print document, your grid might specify the default locations of footers and headers, page numbers, and rules, as well as the width of margins and columns. On a Web site, your page grid might specify the location of navigation menus, navigation headers and footers, page headings, and body text. In most word processing programs and Web editors, such as Microsoft Word and FrontPage, the page grid is not displayed on the screen unless you are editing a header or footer or formatting text in columns. In most desktop publishing programs, such as Adobe PageMaker and Microsoft Publisher, the grid is visible as a set of faint dotted lines on each page.

7b White Space

White space—literally, blank space—frames and separates elements on a page. For example, you would place more white space above a major heading than below it to show that the heading is related to the text below it. White space framing—or surrounding—an illustration and its caption

How to Set Up Pages

To set up pages in Microsoft Word, choose the `File > Page Setup` command from the main menu. Among other options, the Page Setup dialog box allows you to specify page margins, page orientation, paper size and source, and header and footer locations.

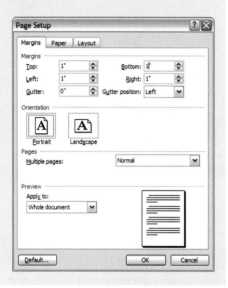

shows that the caption and illustration are a unit separate from nearby or surrounding text.

White space plays an additional role in documents created for classes, such as essays. Wide margins surrounding the text on the page provide space for instructors to comment on print essays.

7c Margins and Gutters

A margin is the white space between the edge of the page or screen (top, bottom, right, and left) and the beginning of the text or graphics in your document. A gutter is the white space between two facing pages that is set aside for documents that will be bound. Margins and gutters are defined by your page grid. You can use these elements to control the placement of text, illustrations, and other objects on the page or screen.

In most word processing and desktop publishing programs, you can set the margins using menu commands or the ruler, which typically appears at the top and sometimes to the left of the word processing window. You can format parts of your document so they have larger or smaller right and/or left margins than the rest of your text. This is useful for setting off long quotations, calling attention to specific passages of text, and setting text outside the standard margins (as is often done for pull quotes—quotations that are pulled out from the rest of the text—in magazine and newspaper articles).

7d Columns

Columns provide additional design opportunities, allowing you greater control over where to place illustrations and other elements on a page. Essays are typically formatted in a single column, whereas newspaper and magazine articles—and, to a growing extent, articles published on the Web—are usually formatted in multiple columns. Columns serve two general purposes.

How to Format Margins

To format margins in Microsoft Word, use one of the following techniques:

Menu Commands Choose the `File > Page Setup` command from the main menu. The Page Setup dialog box allows you to specify top, left, bottom, and right margins. You can also set a *gutter*—the white space between two facing pages that is set aside for documents that will be bound. The Page Setup dialog box also allows you to set the orientation of the page and apply margin settings to the entire document or to everything following your current location in the document.

Using Rulers If your ruler is not already visible, you can display it using the `View > Ruler` command from the main menu. Select the text for which you want to change the margins, or choose the `Edit > Select All` command from the main menu to set the margins for the entire document. To set right and left margins, move your mouse over the margin indicator on the horizontal ruler (the gray area to the left and right of the ruler), click, and drag it to the desired setting. To set top and bottom margins, move your mouse over the margin indicator on the vertical ruler, click, and drag it to the desired setting.

They can improve the readability of a document by limiting the physical movement of the eyes across the page. By limiting the width of a column of text to the amount of space that the eyes can focus on without having to move left or right a great deal, readers can work through a document more quickly. To test this, compare the time and effort it takes to read text on a Web page formatted in a narrow column with text on a Web page that spans an entire screen. Reading—particularly on a large screen—is noticeably faster when the text is formatted in columns.

Columns also simplify some design decisions related to the placement of illustrations and sidebars. Consider the design of the essay in Figure 7.1 and the article in Figure 7.2, which use columns in strikingly different ways. In the academic essay and *The New Republic* article, which are both formatted in two columns, the columns provide a foundation for the other design elements on the pages. In the essay in

Learn about using illustrations on p. 77, sidebars on p. 56, and pull quotes on p. 54.

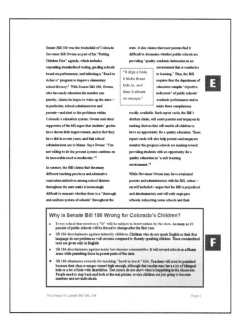

Figure 7.1   An academic essay formatted in columns.

A The title spans two columns.

B A drop cap—a single letter that spans two or more lines of text (see p. 56)—serves as decoration.

C A footer identifies the essay title, author, and page number.

D A photograph and caption identify a major supporter of the bill.

E A pull quote calls attention to opposition to the bill.

F A sidebar lists reasons to oppose the bill.

Figure 7.1, a photograph and caption are positioned in the right column. In contrast, in *The New Republic* article, an image is centered and wrapped by two columns. Also, in the academic essay, additional design elements—two pull quotes and a sidebar—emerge from the grid created by its two-column layout (see Fugure 7.2).

The column layout in the article published by Salon.com (see Figure 7.3) functions in a manner different from that of the academic essay and magazine article. The article itself is laid out in a single column, with related material, ads, and navigation tools displayed in the left and right columns. In addition to simplifying the process of reading the article, this layout clearly distinguishes the site content (the article itself) from its supporting materials (navigation and advertisements).

Most word processing and desktop publishing programs allow you to create two or more columns of text on a single page. You can also achieve this effect (although with much more effort) on a Web page by creating a table and placing text directly into it.

Figure 7.2 Article in *The New Republic*. This article uses a simple layout: a two-column layout broken up by the headline and a single image. Drop caps provide some variety. (*Source: The New Republic*, February 24, 2003, pp. 20–21)

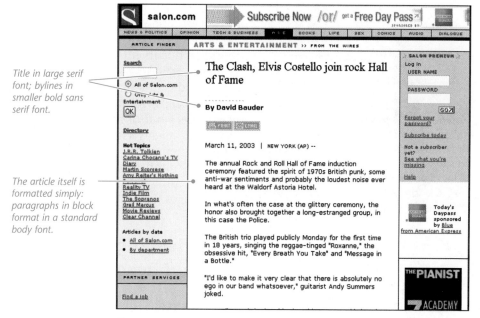

Title in large serif font; bylines in smaller bold sans serif font.

The article itself is formatted simply: paragraphs in block format in a standard body font.

Figure 7.3 Article in Salon.com. This article is presented within a sandwich of site information, promotional materials, and a login form. (*Source:* Salon.com, March 11, 2003)

How to Format Columns

You can format columns in Microsoft Word by using one of the following techniques:

Menu Commands Choose the `Format > Columns` command from the main menu. You can specify the number of columns, their width, and the spacing between them. You can apply your column settings to the entire document, to just the text you select, or to all text after your current location in the document.

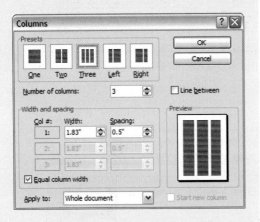

Toolbar Buttons Click on the columns icon in the toolbar and drag the mouse across the dropdown box to choose the number of columns you want. If you have not selected any text, the formatting will be applied to the entire document.

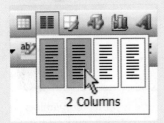

7e Page Numbers, Headers, and Footers

Page numbers, headers, and footers—text that appears at the top or bottom of the page in a location set apart from the main text—serve several functions in print and digital documents. They help readers find their way through a document; they can provide important information about the content of particular sections of a document; and they often help to frame a page visually. Page numbers, when they appear by themselves, help the reader understand where he or she is in a document (particularly useful in longer documents). Headers and footers, which typically include page numbers, also serve this purpose. They can also provide additional information about the document, such as its title, current section or chapter in longer documents, publication date, and author.

Periodicals—magazines, newspapers, journals, newsletters—typically use headers and/or footers. So do most academic essays (see Figure 7.4). In longer documents, headers, footers, and page numbers lend a sense of consistency and stability by repeating across pages.

7f Headings and Subheadings

Headings and subheadings signal sections and subsections to your readers. By scanning headings and subheadings, your readers can more easily lo-

Donatelli 3

other younger music lovers, he finds most of his music online, using both file-sharing programs such as

Kazaa and Morpheus (see Table 1) and fee-based online services such as Apple's iTunes, RealNetworks'

Rhapsody, Napster, and AOL's MusicNet, to name only a few (see Figure 1). Why is a new generation of

Figure 7.4 Header in an academic essay. A header appears at the top right of each page in this academic essay. The writer's last name is followed by the page number.

cate information in your document. Headings and subheadings also serve as transitional devices, signaling to your readers that you are shifting from one subject to another. To enhance the effectiveness of your headings, follow these guidelines.

1. **Use font size and effect to clearly distinguish headings and levels of subheadings.** Generally, bigger, bolder fonts are assigned to headings, while successively smaller fonts are assigned to subheadings. By following this general practice, you make it easier for your readers to identify the beginning of major sections and subsections in your document. Figure 7.5 shows the difference between ineffective and effective formatting. Notice how the size and weights of the fonts used for the headings in the example with effective formatting suggest the relative importance of the material in each section.

How to Create and Format Headers, Footers, and Page Numbers

In Microsoft Word, you can create and format headers, footers, and page numbers by choosing the `View > Header and Footer` command from the main menu. This allows you to view the

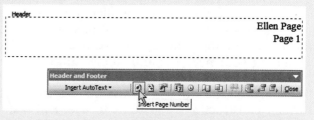

Header and Footer toolbar, with which you can create headers (at the top of the page) and footers (at the bottom of the page). The Header and Footer toolbar allows you to add and edit text and insert page numbers, dates, and times. It also allows you to control the location of the header or footer. This example shows the mouse hovering over the Insert Page Number button.

Ineffective Formatting	Effective Formatting
The Problem The real issue we face is not one that should or could be taken lightly. We must move forward quickly if we are to determine a solution. We must find it within ourselves not only to define the problem but to solve it, and to do so quickly. . . . ## Causes of the Problem The issue must be addressed quickly if we are to be certain that we do not underestimate it. We must look for causes and effects, effects and causes. And we must do so quickly. . . . ### *Lack of Funding* If we are to fund this problem, it must be with current year dollars, not with some sort of promissory note. We must move onward and upward, establishing lines of credit and funding opportunities in a reasonable and straightforward manner. It must be so. Let's make it so. . . . **Lack of Trained Staff** The real problem, of course, is the lack of trained staff. We must find a way to train our people and do so quickly. We must motivate them, train them, work with them, supervise them, house them, feed them, entertain them, and transport them. This is imperative. Really. . . .	**The Problem** The real issue we face is not one that should or could be taken lightly. We must move forward quickly if we are to determine a solution. We must find it within ourselves not only to define the problem but to solve it, and to do so quickly. . . . ***Causes of the Problem*** The issue must be addressed quickly if we are to be certain that we do not underestimate it. We must look for causes and effects, effects and causes. And we must do so quickly. . . . Lack of Funding If we are to fund this problem, it must be with current year dollars, not with some sort of promissory note. We must move onward and upward, establishing lines of credit and funding opportunities in a reasonable and straightforward manner. It must be so. Let's make it so. . . . Lack of Trained Staff The real problem, of course, is the lack of trained staff. We must find a way to train our people and do so quickly. We must motivate them, train them, work with them, supervise them, house them, feed them, entertain them, and transport them. This is imperative. Really. . . .

Figure 7.5 Formatting of headings and subheadings.

2. **Phrase your headings consistently.** Headings and subheadings work together best when they use similar grammatical constructions. Similar constructions — such as a set of questions or a series of statements — are particularly useful for readers who skim a text before they read it carefully. Phrasing your headings and subheadings consistently helps readers better understand the key points and overall organization of a document. To do this, first decide whether to use questions or statements, and then decide which constructions you want to use. For example, all of your headings might be noun phrases, such as "The Problem" and "Possible Solutions to the Problem," or gerund phrases, such as "Defining the Problem" and "Identifying Solutions to the Problem." The examples in Figure 7.6 show the difference between inconsistent and consistent phrasing at the subhead level.

Inconsistent Phrasing

Defining the Problem

The real issue we face is not one that should or could be taken lightly. We must move forward quickly if we are to determine a solution. We must find it within ourselves not only to define the problem but to solve it, and to do so quickly. . . .

What Caused the Problem?

The issue must be addressed quickly if we are to be certain that we do not underestimate it. We must look for causes and effects, effects and causes. And we must do so quickly. . . .

Lack of Funding

If we are to fund this problem, it must be with current year dollars, not with some sort of promissory note. We must move onward and upward, establishing lines of credit and funding opportunities in a reasonable and straightforward manner. It must be so. Let's make it so. . . .

Trained Staff Have Not Been Available

The real problem, of course, is the lack of trained staff. We must find a way to train our people and do so quickly. We must motivate them, train them, work with them, supervise them, house them, feed them, entertain them, and transport them. This is imperative. Really. . . .

Consistent Phrasing

The Problem

The real issue we face is not one that should or could be taken lightly. We must move forward quickly if we are to determine a solution. We must find it within ourselves not only to define the problem but to solve it, and to do so quickly. . . .

Causes of the Problem

The issue must be addressed quickly if we are to be certain that we do not underestimate it. We must look for causes and effects, effects and causes. And we must do so quickly. . . .

Lack of Funding

If we are to fund this problem, it must be with current year dollars, not with some sort of promissory note. We must move onward and upward, establishing lines of credit and funding opportunities in a reasonable and straightforward manner. It must be so. Let's make it so. . . .

Lack of Trained Staff

The real problem, of course, is the lack of trained staff. We must find a way to train our people and do so quickly. We must motivate them, train them, work with them, supervise them, house them, feed them, entertain them, and transport them. This is imperative. Really. . . .

Figure 7.6 Phrasing of headings and subheadings.

3. **Use the Styles tool to ensure consistent formatting.** One of the best ways to ensure consistent formatting of headings and subheadings is to use the Styles tool in your word processing or desktop publishing program. Styles are collections of formatting choices that you can apply, in a single step, to text in your document. Most word processing or desktop publishing programs and Web editors have built-in styles, such as Heading 1, Heading 2, Heading 3, normal paragraph format, emphasis, and so on. Some styles, such as emphasis, are **character** styles that can be applied to individual characters, words, and sentences. To apply a character style, select the text and then choose the style. Other styles, such as headings, are **paragraph** styles that affect all text in a paragraph. To apply a paragraph style, place your cursor somewhere in the paragraph and then choose the style.

How to Create and Modify Styles

In Microsoft Word, you can create styles by using the Styles and Formatting task pane. To view the task pane, use the `Format > Styles and Formatting` command from the main menu.

To create a new style, click on the New Style button in the Styles and Formatting task pane. The New Style dialog box will appear.

To modify a style, place your mouse cursor over its name in the Styles and Formatting task pane, click on the down arrow that appears, and choose Modify. The Modify Style dialog box will appear.

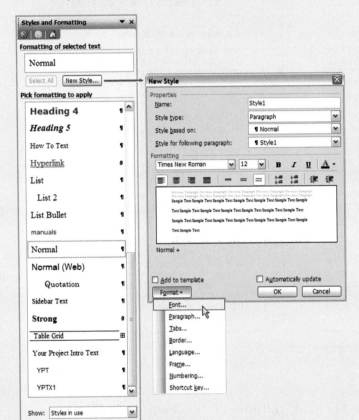

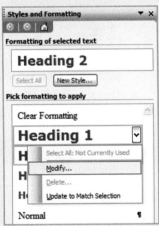

How to Apply Styles

To apply styles in Microsoft Word, use one of the following techniques:

Toolbar Buttons To apply a style using the Formatting toolbar, select the text you want to format, then click on the Styles list. The list of available styles will open. Click on the style you want to use.

Task Pane To apply a style using the Styles and Formatting task pane, select the text you want to format, and then click on the style you want to use in the list displayed in the task pane.

The Styles tool in Microsoft Word allows you to assign specific formatting commands to a style, such as Heading 1, Heading 2, or Heading 3. You can define a style for each level of heading in your document by using such formatting commands as font size, typeface, and effect, as well as spacing, indentation, and color.

7g   Bulleted and Numbered Lists

A bulleted or numbered list displays brief passages of related information using symbols or numbers. The white space surrounding the list draws the eye to the list, highlighting the information for your readers, and typically making that information easier to understand. Bulleted and numbered lists are particularly useful in documents that present information in discrete chunks and/or documents that are likely to be skimmed, such as multimedia reports, Web sites, reports, memos, and instruction manuals. Use numbered lists when sequence is important, such as instructions for an activity or an outline of a series of events. Use bulleted lists when the items in the list are of roughly equal importance. For example, on your résumé your accomplishments can be highlighted in bulleted lists below each heading (see Figure 7.7).

Bulleted List

> **Accomplishments:**
> - Increased sales by 17 percent over the previous year
> - Led development of new marketing plan
> - Identified new sales prospects

Numbered List

> How to fly:
> 1. Watch a bird.
> 2. Be the bird.
> 3. Flap your arms briskly.
> 4. Leave the ground.
> 5. Stay off the ground.

Figure 7.7 Bulleted and numbered lists.

How to Create Bulleted and Numbered Lists

To create bulleted and numbered lists in Microsoft Word, select the text or place your cursor in the paragraph you want to convert to a list, and then use one of the following techniques:

Menu Commands Choose the Format > Bullets and Numbering command from the main menu. You can also select the Bullets and Numbering command with your mouse by right clicking (Windows) or control clicking (Macintosh).

Toolbar Buttons Click on the bulleted or numbered list toolbar icon to create a bulleted or numbered list.

Keyboard Commands You can create a list by typing a number or an asterisk followed by a tab indent at the beginning of a line. When you begin a new line (by pressing the ENTER key), Microsoft Word will convert the line to a bulleted or numbered list.

7h   Captions and Bylines

Captions describe or explain an illustration, such as a photograph or chart. They are usually placed below the illustration and, in MLA and APA styles, are numbered. The first word in a caption should always be capitalized. Punctuation is needed at the end of a caption if it is a complete sentence, but incomplete sentences do not need a period. Bylines, which are often used in articles and opinion columns to identify authors, are usually placed near the beginning of the body text. Captions and bylines are usually formatted in a different style than the body text. If the body text uses a regular serif typeface, for example, a caption might use an italic sans serif font and a byline might use boldface (see Figure 7.8).

7i   Marginal Glosses and Pull Quotes

Marginal glosses are brief notes in a margin that explain or expand on text in the body of the document. Authors use them for purposes such as defining an unfamiliar term or concept used in the text, identifying the source of information used in the body of the text, commenting on a key point in the body text, or referring the reader to related material elsewhere in the docu-

Figure 7.8 Article byline and caption. A byline (**A**) and a photo caption (**B**) formatted to distinguish them from the body text of an article. (*Source: Time,* September 15, 2003, pp. 68–69)

Figure 7.9 Pull quote in an article. A pull quote is set off from the main body of the document in a larger font and different color. (*Source: Real Simple,* April 2003, p. 226)

ment or in other sources. Well-designed marginal glosses usually use a different font from that used for the body text—often a smaller point size in boldface or a contrasting color.

Pull quotes highlight a particular passage of text—frequently a quotation made by a key figure discussed in the article—by pulling it out of the main body of the text and highlighting it (see Figure 7.9). Writers use pull quotes to call attention to a particularly important fact or quotation, provide a

How to Create and Format Text Boxes

Text boxes allow you to create passages of text and graphics that can be moved around the screen independently of your margins. Text boxes can be formatted with borders, shading, and colors, and they can be placed in front of or behind text on a page. A text box can also be set so that text wraps around it. In Microsoft Word, you can create and format text boxes using the following techniques:

Creating Text Boxes

Menu Commands Choose the `Insert > Text Box` command from the main menu. In your document, click and drag your mouse across the area where you want to create the text box.

Toolbar Buttons On the Drawing toolbar, click on the Text Box icon. In your document, click and drag your mouse across the area where you want to create the text box. If the Drawing toolbar is not showing, right click (Windows) or control click (Macintosh) with your mouse on any visible toolbar and click the box next to "Drawing."

Formatting Text Boxes

Menu Commands To format a text box using the main menu, click on the text box and then choose the `Format > Text Box` command. The Format Text Box dialog box will appear. You can also right click (Windows) or control click (Macintosh) on the border of the text box and select the `Format > Text Box` command. The dialog box allows you to format the fill colors, border, size, layout, internal margins, and internal text wrapping options. If the layout options are set so that text wraps around the text box, you can move the text box to different locations on the page by clicking and dragging.

Toolbar Buttons To format a text box using the Drawing toolbar, select the text box and use the icons on the toolbar. The icons allow you to change the border color, fill color, border thickness and style, 3D options, and shadow effects. If the Drawing toolbar is not showing, right click (Windows) or control click (Macintosh) with your mouse on any visible toolbar, and click the box next to "Drawing."

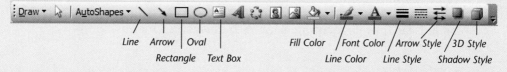

statement that summarizes a main or supporting point in a document, or entertain readers with a light or humorous quote. Pull quotes are typically displayed in a different font and often in a different color from the body text.

You can create pull quotes and marginal glosses in most word processing programs by using text boxes (see p. 55) and formatting the text box so that it appears in the margin or is wrapped by body text.

7j   Sidebars

Sidebars are brief discussions of information related to but not a central part of your document. Sidebars simplify the task of integrating related or supporting information into the body of the article by setting that information off in a clearly defined area. Newspaper and magazine articles frequently include sidebars, while articles published on the Web typically do not. Instead, Web-based articles are more likely to provide a link to a pop-up window or to another page containing the related information. The academic essay in Figure 7.1 (p. 46) contains a sidebar on the bottom of the second page. As is typically the case with sidebars, the text is bordered and shaded so that it stands out from the main text of the article.

You can create sidebars in most word processing programs by using text boxes (see p. 55) and formatting the text box so that body text wraps around it or breaks before and after it. You can use the borders and shading tools to distinguish your sidebar from the body text of the document.

7k   Decorative Elements

Decorative items, such as drop caps and logos, add visual interest to a text. They often serve to break up longer passages of body text. They can also signal to the reader the beginning of an article or a major section. Logos are small images related to the publication in which a document appears, such as a magazine or Web site. Drop caps are a single capital letter at the beginning of a paragraph that precedes two or more lines of text (see a drop cap in an essay in Figure 7.1 on p. 46 and in an article in Figure 7.2 on p. 47).

7l   Examples: Alternative Page Layouts

Your choices about page layout can affect the readability and attractiveness of your document. Inadequate line spacing, for example, will create the appearance of dense, crowded text—perhaps so crowded that the words on the page will be difficult to make out. Similarly, using different page grids within the same document will make it harder for readers to locate navigation aids such as page numbers or Web navigation menus.

Figures 7.10, 7.11, and 7.12, which all show the opening page of an informative article about the Intensive English Program at Colorado State University, illustrate the effects of alternative decisions about page layout.

Figure 7.10 Crowded page design.

The page is crowded, uses very little white space, and is less readable than the examples in Figures 7.11 and 7.12.

A *The margins of this document are tight, contributing to the crowded feeling.*

B *Line spacing is 11 points, making the text difficult to read.*

C *Body text is fully justified and presented in a single column, making the text difficult to read because the spacing between words is uneven and the lines of text are extremely long.*

D *No extra space between paragraphs.*

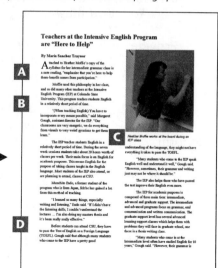

Figure 7.11 Open, more readable page design.

The more open layout of this page increases the readability of the document.

A *Ample margins.*

B *The line spacing is a reader-friendly 15 points.*

C *Body text is left aligned and presented in a single column.*

D *Six points of extra space between paragraphs.*

Figure 7.12 Open, more readable page design using columns.

This document uses a two-column layout to increase the amount of white space on the page.

A *Ample margins.*

B *The line spacing is a reader-friendly 15 points.*

C *Body text is left aligned and presented in two columns. Photograph is reduced in size to fit the column width.*

D *Six points of extra space between paragraphs.*

Typically, writers have greater control over page layout in print documents. However, the growing sophistication of Web design tools, such as Macromedia Dreamweaver and Microsoft FrontPage, and the built-in HTML conversion tools in many word processing programs have given writers more control over the layout of Web pages.

7m Page Layout Guidelines

Consider the following guidelines as you create your page layouts.

1. Create a common page grid for your document. A common page grid will provide a similar look and feel to the pages in your document. It will also help your readers more easily identify the locations of recurring elements, such as page headers and footers and Web navigation menus. However, don't be a slave to your page grid. To create variety across your pages, it's useful to depart in minor ways from the common page grid on some of the pages in your document. Many newsletters, magazines, newspapers, and Web sites, for example, will vary their pages to adapt to the specific needs of the material on a page.

2. Provide appropriate margins. Consider how readers will use your document. If you are writing an academic essay, leave plenty of room for classmates and instructors to write marginal comments. If you are planning to bind your document, leave enough space for the binding.

3. Use white space to call attention to important elements on the page. White space can identify the beginning of major sections and call out key ideas and information. Add extra space before major headings, and use white space to set off illustrations, pull quotes, and marginal glosses.

4. Provide sufficient line spacing to make text readable. Compressed lines of text are difficult to read. Help your readers stay focused by providing enough space between lines to ease the reading process.

5. Use numbered and bulleted lists to chunk and call attention to information. Lists direct your readers to key information in a compact, easy-to-read form.

6. Avoid wide columns of text. The physical act of moving your eyes across long lines of text makes a document more difficult to read. Consider narrower columns on Web pages and in magazine and newspaper articles.

7. Enhance readability by using left aligned body text. Fully justified text (text that is aligned to the right and left margins of a page or column) is often created by adding unequal spacing between words and even between letters. Most academic essays, for example, are easier to read when they are left aligned and ragged right.

8. **Signal the functions of text by varying its format and color.** Use text formatting to distinguish bylines, captions, headings, block quotes, pull quotes, headers, footers, and sidebars from the body text of your pages.

9. **When appropriate, use decorative elements, such as drop caps, to add variety and interest to your pages.**

Design Activity

Analyzing Design *Find a magazine, such as* Time *or* Newsweek, *that uses a variety of layouts for its articles. Alternatively, find a Web site that has pages with varying layouts. Cut out, photocopy, or print the articles or Web pages and analyze their layouts.*

1. *On each page, locate and annotate the elements that are discussed in this chapter: white space, margins and gutters, columns, headers and footers, page numbers, headings and subheadings, bulleted and numbered lists, captions and bylines, marginal glosses and pull quotes, sidebars, and drop caps.*

2. *Using a marker, sketch the page grid for each page. Compare the page grids to determine whether they are fundamentally different or variations on a shared grid.*

3. *Write a brief analysis of the layout of one of the pages, identifying effective uses of the elements discussed in this chapter and critiquing ineffective uses of those elements.*

Applying Design *Locate an academic essay you've written for a class. Using what you've learned from your analysis, create a new page grid for the essay. Create a copy of the document and reformat it to conform to your new page grid, adding design elements such as headers and footers, pull quotes, marginal glosses, sidebars, and drop caps. Write a brief analysis of the impact your new page grid has on the essay's effectiveness and usability.*

CHAPTER 8

Navigation Aids

I f you have written a long, complicated document, your readers may find it difficult to locate specific information in it. In longer print documents and digital documents with a linear structure similar to a series of pages in a book (such as word processing files and Adobe® Acrobat files), you can help your readers locate information by providing tables of contents, indexes, and marginal and in-text cross references. On Web sites, you can create navigation menus (such as button bars and dropdown menus), navigation headers and footers, graphical site maps, search tools, links, tables of contents, and indexes.

8a Navigation Tools for Print Documents

Tables of contents and indexes are frequently included in longer print documents, such as reports and manuals. Word processing programs allow you to automatically create these navigation aids, but only if you've used the Styles formatting tool in your document. If you haven't used the Styles tool, you can reformat your document relatively quickly in most word processing programs (see p. 51). Print documents also use marginal cross references and in-text cross references. The "see p. 51" in this paragraph is an example of an in-text cross reference. The "learn about formatting styles" reference in the margin of this paragraph is an example of a marginal cross reference. In-text cross references can be inserted anywhere in your document, and you can create marginal cross references in most word processing programs by using text boxes.

Learn about using styles on p. 52 and text boxes on p. 55.

8b Navigation Tools for the Web

If you are developing a Web site, your choice of navigational tools depends on the size and complexity of your site, its organizational structure (see p. 115), and your readers' familiarity with the Web. At a minimum, you should provide links to and from related pages. However, there are advantages to providing additional support, including tables of contents, indexes, graphical site maps, navigation side menus, navigation headers and footers, and search tools.

Links   On the Web, links function in three ways. Internal links move you to a new location on the current page you are viewing. External links replace the current page with a new page, either within the current Web site or elsewhere. Pop-up links open a new document in a new browser window. Web

How to Create and Edit Links

Most word processing and desktop publishing programs—and all Web editors—allow you to create links between documents. In many programs, you can also create links within a document (such as from a table of contents to a location elsewhere in the document). To create and edit links in Microsoft Word, use these techniques:

Creating and Formatting New Links Select the text or object (picture, text box, graphic object) that you want to link and then choose the `Insert > Hyperlink` command from the main menu or the Insert Hyperlink icon in the toolbar. The Insert Hyperlink dialog box allows you to select a destination (a file or a Web location) or to type a URL in the Address field. You can also create informational flags (which appear when a mouse cursor is placed over a link) by clicking on the Screen Tip button. The Target Frame button allows you to choose whether to open the document in the current window or in a new window. Other options, such as linking within the document or creating a link to an e-mail address, are also available.

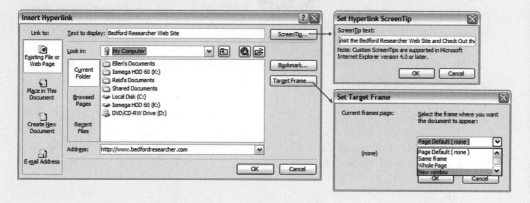

Formatting Existing Links
To format an existing hyperlink, right click (Windows) or control click (Macintosh) on the link and select the `Edit Hyperlink` command. The Edit Hyperlink dialog box, which is similar in appearance to the Insert Hyperlink dialog box, will appear, allowing you to format the link.

Figure 8.1 Internal links on a Web page. Links appear as a table of contents near the beginning of the page.

Reflections on Youth Voting Patterns

As the Vietnam War raged, younger Americans – and many who were not so young – lobbied vigorously and ultimately successfully for changes in the voting age. In the 1970s, the voting age was lowered from 21 to 18. Although hailed as a reasonable response to a nation that viewed 18-year-olds as mature enough to go to war, the change has had little impact on election outcomes in the United State. Or has it? This essay explores some of the predictable and unpredictable outcomes of the change.

- Introduction
- History: The Vietnam War and U.S. Concepts of Adult Responsibilities
- History: A Battle Won – 18-Year-Olds Go to the Polls Assessment: Youth Voting Patters since 1976
- Implications: A Lost Generation after Generation after Generation?
- Moving Ahead: Rethinking the Voting Age?

Introduction

Figure 8.2 Graphical site map of the U.S. Environmental Protection Agency Web site.

(*Source:* Environmental Protection Agency, http://www.epa.gov/emap/html/sitemap.html)

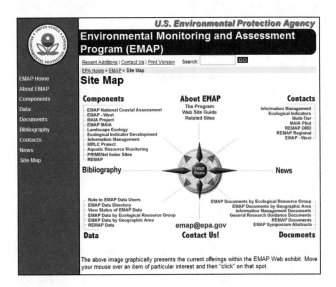

editing programs allow you to create links in several ways: **text links** that open when you click on linked words in the text of the document; **links lists** that typically appear as a menu, index, or table of contents; **image links** that open when you click on an image; and **button links** that open when you click on a button.

If you are developing a single-page document online, you will most likely provide a set of internal links to sections of that page and, perhaps, a set of external links to related pages elsewhere on the Web. Your links might appear as a list similar to a table of contents (see Figure 8.1). If you are developing a site with multiple pages, you will most likely provide a navigation menu that will help readers move from page to page within the site.

Tables of Contents, Indexes, and Graphical Site Maps   If you are creating a site with multiple pages, you can use tables of contents and indexes, which are often similar to those found in print documents, to help even readers who are relatively unfamiliar with the Web locate information on your site. You can also use a site map—a graphical representation of key pages on your site (see Figure 8.2). Sites maps are useful because most people are familiar with road maps. By laying out the overall organization of your site, a site map can help readers understand both the content and the structure of your site.

Side Menus   Buttons or links that appear along the side of a Web page can make it easier for your readers to find their way around your site. Side menus, usually prominently displayed on each page in the site, help readers understand the site's contents and structure at a glance (see Figure 8.3).

How to Create Tables of Contents

Microsoft Word lets you create a table of contents with its built-in Styles (Heading 1, Heading 2, Heading 3, and so on), by using your own styles, or by marking locations within the document. To create a table of contents in Microsoft Word, follow these steps:

1. Place your cursor at the point in your document where you want the table of contents to appear.

2. Choose the `Insert > Reference > Index and Tables` command from the main menu to open the Index and Tables dialog box.

3. Select the Table of Contents tab. You can now choose the format for your table of contents, select the styles you will use to build your table, and preview the appearance of the table in print and Web documents.

To learn how to create a table of contents without using Styles, search for "table of contents" in Word's online help.

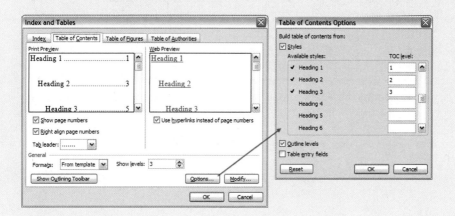

Navigation Headers and Footers   Navigation headers are a line of links running along the top of a page. Some navigation headers indicate where the reader is within the site's structure (see Figure 8.3). Navigation footers are a set of links running along the bottom of the page. They typically provide access to pages containing information about the site itself, such as contact information and copyright statements. Navigation footers can also provide links to main pages on the site, usually in the form of text links.

Search Tools   Search tools can be similar to those found on major search sites, such as Google or Yahoo! These tools provide access to either the Web or to material found only on the current site. Search tools have become extremely easy to add to a Web site or page. Google, for instance, allows you to fill out a simple form that gives you permission to use Google to search your site. You can copy the result—a few lines of code—and insert it into your Web page.

A navigation header, with links to major sections of the site, appears on the top of each page.

Site search form.

A side menu can be found on the left side of each page on The New Republic Online site.

A navigation footer appears on the bottom of each page.

Link to article on another page.

Figure 8.3 Navigation tools on a Web site. (*Source:* The New Republic Online, http://tnr.com)

Design Activity

Locate a longer print document, such as a textbook or an instruction manual, or a larger Web site. Do the following:

1. *Identify the likely readers of the document. For example, the readers of a textbook might be college students majoring in biology, while the readers of an instruction manual might be people who have just purchased a new software program.*

2. *List the navigation tools used to help readers locate information in the document.*

3. *Rate the usefulness of each navigation tool on a 10-point scale, with 10 being most useful.*

4. *Provide a brief justification for each rating.*

5. *Write a brief assessment of the document's use of navigation tools. If appropriate, recommend the use of different or additional navigation tools.*

CHAPTER 9

Color

Color is an important, but frequently underused, design element. Two factors, however, have dramatically increased the use of color in documents produced in academic, business, and personal settings. First, word processing, desktop publishing, and Web design programs have become more sophisticated and easier to use. Writers, as a result, have been able to incorporate color into their documents with greater ease than they could in the past. Second, the cost of color inkjet and laser printers has decreased dramatically, allowing more writers to create high-quality color documents.

Your choices about color can have surprisingly different effects on readers. Some of these effects are physical. Yellow, for example, is a relatively bright color. Web pages that use a bright yellow background can tire your readers' eyes. Other effects are emotional and are often linked to your readers' cultural backgrounds. In many cultures, green is considered soothing. It is often associated with nature and growth. Red, in contrast, is associated in a number of cultures with danger. As a result, it tends to attract a reader's attention. As you work with color, consider both the physical and emotional effects your choices are likely to have on your readers.

In general, color can be used to do the following:

- Call attention to important information in your document.
- Signal your overall organizational scheme through the use of color in headings and subheadings.
- Signal the function of particular types of text in your document, such as long quotations, pull quotes, bylines, and captions.
- Increase the overall attractiveness of your document.

9a Calling Attention to Important Information

Used appropriately, color can increase the attractiveness of and call attention to specific parts of a document. Consider, for example, Figure 9.1, which shows the same article in black and white and in color.

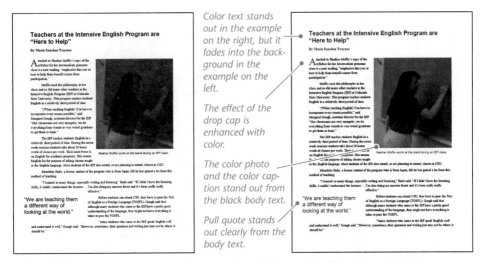

Figure 9.1 Using color to call attention to important information in an article.

9b Signaling the Organization of a Document

Color can also signal the organization of a document. In a longer print document—such as a report, a manual, or a book—a header or footer might be formatted with a particular color. Headings and subheadings in that section might also be formatted in that color, further signaling to readers which section they are viewing (see Figure 9.2). On a Web site, a similar color coding effect might be created by formatting pages in a particular section with a specific background color. Those colors could be shown in a navigation side menu displayed on every page in the site, helping readers recognize which section they are currently viewing (see Figure 9.3).

Section 4: New Approaches to Digital Music   Page 56

the current legislative agenda suggests that we are facing the end of music distribution as it has commonly been carried out in the United States.

Leading Models for Distributing Music Online

Three major approaches to fee-based digital distribution of music have been attempted over the past seven years. These include subscription services, license-based retail purchases, and a combined subscription-

---

Figure 9.2 Color-coded sections in a print document.

How to Format Color

In Microsoft Word, you can format the color of text, autoshapes, and page backgrounds by using the following techniques:

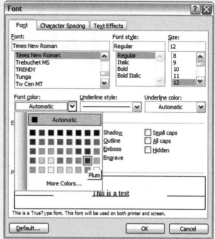

Text Select the text you want to format in color. Choose the `Format > Font` command from the main menu to display the Font dialog box. You can also choose the `Font` command with your mouse by right clicking (Windows) or control clicking (Macintosh). Click on the Font color dropdown box to open the color picker and select the color you wish to apply to the text. If you have underlined the text, you can also select a color for the underline.

To format selected text using the Formatting toolbar, click on the Font Color icon and choose a color from the dropdown box. Once you have chosen a color, it will stay active on the toolbar. To apply the same color to other text, click on the icon.

Autoshapes To format the color of autoshapes (rectangles, circles, lines, and other shapes created with Microsoft Word's drawing tools), select the object or autoshape and use the `Format > AutoShape` commands on the main menu. You can also use these commands by right clicking (Windows) or control clicking (Macintosh) on the object or autoshape. The Format AutoShape or Format Object dialog box will allow you to format the fill color and line color.

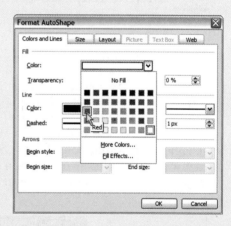

Choose the Colors and Lines tab in the dialog box, and then click on the Fill or Line color dropdowns. You can also use the Color icons on the Drawing toolbar to format objects or autoshapes.

Page Backgrounds Choose the `Format > Background` command from the main menu to choose background colors for pages in a document.

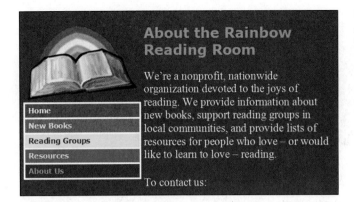

Figure 9.3 Color-coded sections on a Web site.

9c Signaling the Function of Text

Color can help readers recognize the function of text in your document. For example, you can use a colored background to indicate that a passage of text is a sidebar (see Figure 3.3, p. 22), a caption for an illustration or a byline (see Figure 7.8, p. 54); a quotation or a pull quote (see Figure 7.9, p. 54); or a heading or subheading (see Figure 3.1, p. 21). By formatting specific types of text in color, you can distinguish them from body text and other types of text.

9d Color Guidelines

Color can be a valuable tool for highlighting information, helping readers find their way around a document and signaling the function of particular types of text. As you work with color, keep the following guidelines in mind.

1. **Use color consistently.** Use the same colors for top-level headings throughout your document, another color for lower-level headings, and so on. Don't mix and match.

2. **Make sure you have sufficient contrast between your colors.** For instance, avoid using light colors on white or light-colored backgrounds and avoid using red or blue on dark-colored backgrounds.

3. **Restrain yourself.** Avoid using more than three colors on a page unless you are using a photograph or work of art. Don't use a vast array of colors in your print documents just because you have access to a color printer. Similarly, be careful not to scare off readers of your Web page with a jarring array of colors. Use your colors for effect, not just because you know color-formatting commands. Figures 9.4 and 9.5 provide examples of color used well and poorly on a Web site.

Too many colors are used on the page, making it difficult to read and navigate.

Different colors might confuse the reader about the purposes of these links.

The black body text is difficult to read against the dark background.

Figure 9.4 Web site that uses color ineffectively.

Link to a document on another site.

Color is used to call attention to important information, including headings and links to other Web pages.

Links to other pages on the site.

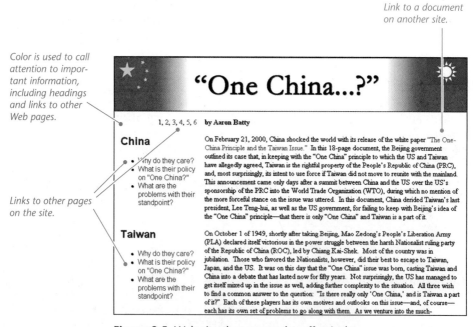

Figure 9.5 Web site that uses color effectively.

Design Activity

Analyzing Design *Locate a document that uses color, such as a magazine article, an essay you've written for another class, a Web site, a brochure or flyer, or a multimedia presentation. Do the following:*

1. *Create a list of design elements in the document that use color, such as headings and subheadings, drop caps, captions, or pull quotes.*

2. *Next to each entry in your list, rate the effectiveness of the use of color on a 10-point scale, with 10 being most effective. As you consider your rating, decide whether the use of color draws the reader's eye to important information or distracts the reader from more important information. Determine as well whether the use of color helps the reader understand the overall organization of the document or signals the function of elements on the page.*

3. *Provide a brief justification for each rating.*

4. *Write a brief analysis of the use of color in the document, identifying effective uses and critiquing ineffective uses.*

Applying Design *Locate an academic essay you've written for a class. The essay should be formatted in black and white. Create a copy of the document, and, using what you've learned from your analysis, reformat the essay in color. Write a brief analysis of the impact color has on the reformatted essay's effectiveness and usability.*

CHAPTER 10

Shading, Borders, and Rules

S hading, borders, and rules (lines running horizontally or vertically on a page) can help readers locate key information and use a document more efficiently. These design elements can be used individually or in combination to do the following:

- Call attention to important information in your document.
- Signal the function of particular types of text in your document, such as sidebars and pull quotes.
- Signal transitions in a document, such as the end of one section and the beginning of the next.
- Increase the overall attractiveness of your document.

10a Calling Attention to Important Information

A combination of borders and shading can subtly yet clearly emphasize an illustration, such as a table or chart, by distinguishing it from the surrounding body text. Similarly, an important passage or list can be pulled into a box and set off from the body text. You'll find this technique used on Web sites and in instruction manuals, as well as in many how-to articles in magazines and newspapers.

10b Signaling the Function of Text

Shading, borders, and rules can be used to distinguish the functions of sections of text in your document. For example, you can use rules above and below a pull quote to differentiate it from other text on a page or screen (see

How to Format Borders and Shading

To format the borders and shading of text, objects and autoshapes, and pages in Microsoft Word, use one of the following techniques:

Text To format the borders and shading of text, select the text you want to format (or place your mouse cursor within a paragraph) and choose the `Format > Borders and Shading` command from the main menu. The Borders and Shading dialog box will open. Select the Borders tab to format the color and weight of the border; select the Shading tab to format the shade and color within the box.

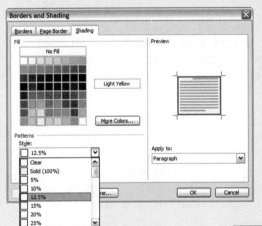

Objects and Autoshapes To format the borders and shading of objects and auto-shapes (rectangles, circles, lines, and other shapes created with Microsoft Word's drawing tools), select the object or autoshape and follow the preceding instructions for formatting the borders and shading the text.

Page Borders To format the borders and shade the page, choose the `Format > Borders and Shading` command from the main menu. The Borders and Shading dialog box will open. You can use the Page Border tab of the Borders and Shading dialog box to format page borders, indicating their color, line thickness, and artistic effects. The border can be applied to all pages in a document or to only pages in a specific section.

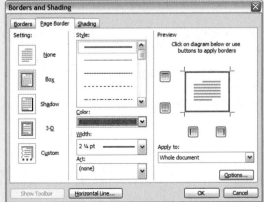

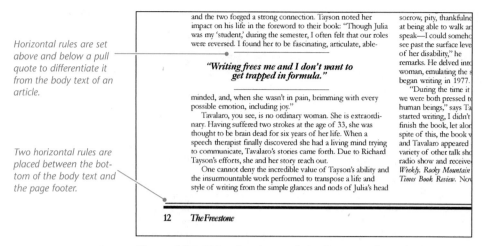

Horizontal rules are set above and below a pull quote to differentiate it from the body text of an article.

Two horizontal rules are placed between the bottom of the body text and the page footer.

Figure 10.1 Using borders and shading to call attention to design elements. (*Source: The Freestone,* English Department, Colorado State University)

Figure 10.1). You can shade a heading or footer to show that it is not part of the body text. Placing the same border around all of the sidebars in an article shows that the text within it is distinct from the body text. You can also use borders and shading to set off navigational tools, such as navigation menus or tables of contents, on a Web site.

10c Signaling Transitions

Rules are particularly useful for signaling the beginning and end of sections of a document or separating passages that serve different functions, such as when a rule appears above information about an author at the end of an article.

10d Shading, Borders, and Rules Guidelines

1. Treat shading, borders, and rules as you would color. They have the same function as color in a document. The cautions about using them, as a result, are the same. Avoid overuse, and make sure you've provided sufficient contrast between your text and background shading.

2. Be aware of the limitations of Web development software. Most word processing and desktop publishing programs provide abundant tools for formatting borders and shading. Web development tools lag behind in this area, largely because of the limitations of the HTML coding language.

However, you can achieve effects similar to those provided by word process-ing and desktop publishing programs by using horizontal rules, tables, and the border and background settings provided through cascading style sheets, a formatting and design specification used to control the appearance of Web pages. (To learn more about cascading style sheets, see Writing the Web: HTML Coding and Web Design at http://www.bedfordresearcher.com/manuals/html/.)

How to Format Vertical and Horizontal Rules

You can create vertical and horizontal rules in Microsoft Word using one of the fol-lowing techniques:

Menu Commands Place your cursor in the text near the location where you want to create a vertical or horizontal rule. Choose the `Format > Borders and Shading` command from the main menu, or choose the `Borders and Shading` command with your mouse by right clicking (Windows) or control clicking (Macintosh). In the Borders and Shading dialog box, select the color and thickness of the line; then click on the top, bottom, or sides of the paragraph icon in the Preview pane to indicate the placement of the line in your document. More stylized horizontal lines can be created by clicking on the Horizontal Line button at the bottom of the Borders and Shading dialog box. By choosing one of the line styles listed in the new dialog box, you can insert a horizontal line at the location of the cursor in your document. To create vertical rules between columns, use the `Format > Columns` command from the main menu.

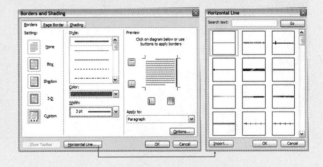

Toolbar Commands You can use the Line tool in the Drawing toolbar to create and format vertical and horizontal rules. Click on the Line tool and draw the line. To con-strain the line to vertical or horizontal directions, hold down the `SHIFT` key as you draw the line. To format the line, first select it, and then set the color and thickness using the Line Color, Line Style, and Dash Style icons on the Drawing toolbar. If the Drawing toolbar is not showing, right click (Windows) or control click (Macintosh) with your mouse on any visible toolbar, and then click the box next to "Drawing."

Line   Arrow   Line Color   Line Style /   Arrow Style
                                                      Dash Style

Design Activity

Analyzing Design *Locate a document with borders, shading, and rules, such as a magazine article, an essay you've written for another class, a Web site, a brochure or flyer, or a multimedia presentation. Do the following:*

1. *Create a list of the design elements that use borders, shading, or rules, such as sidebars, headers and footers, or pull quotes.*

2. *Next to each entry in your list, rate the effectiveness of the use of borders, shading, or rules on a 10-point scale, with 10 being the most effective. As you consider your rating, decide whether the use of borders, shading, or rules draws the reader's eye to important information or distracts the reader from more important information. Determine as well whether their use signals the function of text on the page or signals a transition.*

3. *Provide a brief justification for each rating.*

4. *Write a brief analysis of the use of borders, shading, and rules in the document, identifying effective uses and critiquing ineffective uses.*

Applying Design *Locate an academic essay you've written for a class that does not contain borders, shading, or rules. Create a copy of the document, and, using what you've learned from your analysis, reformat the essay using borders, shading, and rules. Write a brief analysis of the impact these elements have on the reformatted essay's effectiveness and usability.*

CHAPTER 11

Illustrations

Illustrations—photographs and other images, charts, graphs, tables, animations, audio clips, and video clips—can be used to expand on or demonstrate points made in the text of your document. You can use illustrations to demonstrate or emphasize points made in a document, reduce the amount of text needed to make a point, clarify your points, and improve the visual appeal of your document.

11a Photographs and Other Images

Photographs and other images, such as drawings, paintings, and sketches, are frequently used to set a mood, emphasize a point, or demonstrate a point more fully than is possible with text alone. Although readers seldom appreciate the repetition of key points in the text of your document, they welcome well-designed and helpful illustrations that complement descriptions in your text. For example, if you were writing about different kinds of wildflowers, the illustration shown in Figure 11.1 would enhance the written description. Most word processing, desktop publishing, and Web editing programs allow you to insert digitized images directly into a document. If your image has not been digitized, you can use a scanner or digital camera to create an electronic copy and then add it to your document. Although it is usually best to use an image editing program to crop or resize digital images, you can also crop and resize

Figure 11.1 Wildflower illustration. A hand-painted illustration of a wildflower could be used to demonstrate a point made in the text.

How to Insert and Format Images

You can insert and format images of all kinds (photographs, drawings, animations) in Microsoft Word by following these steps:

Inserting Images

1. Place your cursor at the point where you want to insert the image.
2. Choose the `Insert > Picture` command from the main menu.
3. Choose which type of image you wish to insert (Clip Art, File, Scanner or Camera image, New Drawing, and so on).
4. Locate or scan the image you want to insert.
5. Click on OK.

Formatting Images

To format an image that is already in your document, double-click on it. The Format Picture dialog box that opens will allow you to format the size and layout of the image.

within some word processing, desktop publishing, and Web editing programs, such as Microsoft Word, Microsoft Publisher, and Macromedia Dreamweaver.

11b Charts and Graphs

Charts and graphs provide a graphical representation of information. They are typically used to make a point more succinctly than is possible with text alone or to present complex information in a compact and more accessible form. In many cases, a well-designed chart or graph can take the place of several paragraphs of explanatory text. A pie chart, for instance, might illustrate the results of a survey, as shown in Figure 11.2. Charts and graphs can be created with spreadsheet or statistical analysis programs or created within many word processing programs.

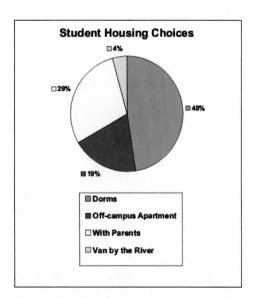

Figure 11.2 Pie chart. A chart often makes a point more succinctly than words.

How to Create and Format Charts and Graphs

To create and format a graph or chart in Microsoft Word, follow these steps:

Creating Charts and Graphs

1. Place your cursor at the point where you want to insert a chart or graph.

2. Choose the `Insert > Picture > Chart` command from the main menu. The menus in Microsoft Word will change, indicating that you are now working on a chart.

3. Select the type of graph or chart you want to display by clicking on the `Chart > Chart Type` command from the main menu.

4. A spreadsheet with data labels and data will open. Replace the data labels and data with your own information.

5. Choose the `File > Update` command from the main menu to insert the chart into your document.

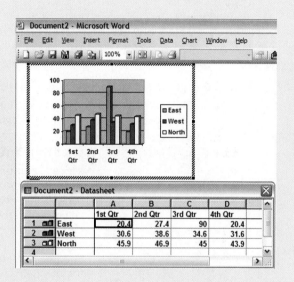

Formatting Charts and Graphs

To format an existing chart or graph, double-click on it. The menus in Microsoft Word will change, indicating that you are now working on the chart or graph.

11c Tables

Tables provide categorical lists of information. Like charts and graphs, they are typically used to make a point more succinctly than is possible with text alone or present complex information in a compact form. Tables can illustrate contrasts between groups, relationships between variables (such as income, educational attainment, and voting preferences), or changes over time (such as growth in population during the past century). A table, for example, might illustrate the results of a survey, as shown in Figure 11.3. Tables are usually created within a word processing program. In some cases, they are generated in a spreadsheet or statistical analysis program and then imported into a document created in a word processing program.

Table 6.2: Software Programs Used by Students at State University to Share Music (Percent by Class)

	Freshmen	Sophomores	Juniors	Seniors
Kazaa	11.2	9.6	8.3	6.2
Morpheus	18.3	19.7	21.6	24.3
Drumbeat	14.5	14.6	15.2	13.9
Grokster	16.8	15.1	14.2	12.8
Piolet	12.3	13.3	14.5	15.0
Overnet	16.9	16.4	14.1	11.7
WinMX	10.0	11.3	12.1	16.1

Figure 11.3 A table provides information organized by categories.

How to Create and Format Tables

To create and format tables in Microsoft Word, place your cursor at the point where you want to insert a table and use one of the following techniques:

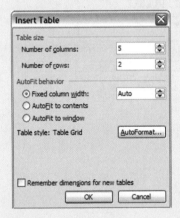

Creating Tables

Menu Commands Choose the `Table > Insert Table` command from the main menu. The Insert Table dialog box will open. Choose the number of columns and rows, set the AutoFit behavior, and click on OK to create the table.

Toolbar Buttons Click on the Table icon on the toolbar, hold down your left mouse button, and drag until you have selected a table with the rows and columns you desire.

Formatting Tables

Using the Tables and Borders Toolbar To format an existing table, display the Tables and Borders toolbar and work with the icons on the

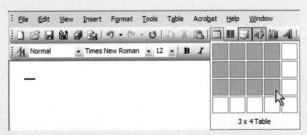

toolbar. If the Tables and Borders toolbar is not showing, right click (Windows) or control click (Macintosh) with your mouse on any visible toolbar, and click the box next to "Tables and Borders."

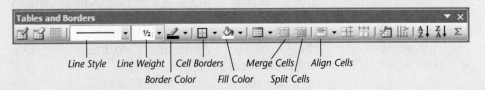

11d Other Digital Illustrations

Digital publications allow you to include a wider range of illustrations, including audio, video, and animations. These illustrations differ from photographs, images, charts, graphs, and tables in that they aren't just there; they *do* things. Audio adds sound to your document, and video and animation supply movement. Although these types of illustrations work only in digital documents (at least until digital paper is perfected), they should not be overlooked as you consider the design of documents such as Web sites and word processing documents.

There are, however, drawbacks to the use of audio, video, and animation in digital documents. Their use can be complicated by factors such as the speed with which your readers will access your document, the capabilities of your readers' computers, and the possibility that animation might distract your readers from the information you want them to read.

How to Insert Animations, Audio Clips, and Video Clips

To insert an animation, audio, or video file in Microsoft Word, follow these steps:

1. Place your cursor at the point where you want to insert an animation, audio, or video file.
2. Choose the `Insert > Object` command from the main menu.
3. Click on the Create from File tab.
4. Click on the Browse button to locate the file you want to insert.
5. Click on OK.

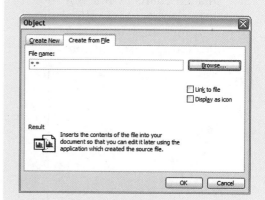

11e Illustrations Guidelines

As word processing, desktop publishing, and Web editing software grows more sophisticated, it continues to be easier to insert and work with illustrations in print and digital documents. Keep the following guidelines in mind as you work with illustrations:

1. **Use an illustration for a purpose.** Illustrations are best used when they serve a clear function in your document. Avoid including illustrations simply because you think they might make your document "look better."

2. **Place illustrations near the text they illustrate.** In general, place illustrations as close as possible to the point where they are mentioned in the

text. If they are not explicitly mentioned (as is often the case with photographs), place them at a point where they will seem most relevant to the information and ideas being discussed.

3. Include a title or caption that identifies or explains the illustration. Although it is not required, it is usually a good idea to include a title or caption. You can find advice on the proper placement and format of titles and captions in the document preparation guidelines provided by organizations such as the Modern Language Association and the American Psychological Association.

4. Consider whether to wrap text around your illustrations or to place them inline. **Wrapping** refers to the practice of allowing text to flow around an illustration. **Inline** placement is letting the illustration interrupt the text without wrapping. Wrapping is typically used for photographs, drawings, and smaller charts, while inline placement is often used for tables and larger illustrations (see Figure 11.4).

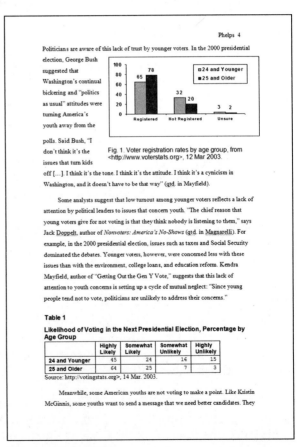

Figure 11.4 Wrapped text. Wrapping allows text to flow around a figure in an essay. A table is placed inline.

Design Activity

Locate an essay or report you've written for another class. Create a copy of the document, and use it to practice inserting illustrations, such as images, tables, charts, and graphs, by doing the following:

1. *Identify locations in the document that would benefit from the insertion of an image, a chart or graph, or a table.*

2. *Provide references to the new illustrations in the text by using a phrase such as "see Figure 3" or "see Table 2."*

3. *Insert an image (photograph or clip art) by following the "How to Insert and Format Images" sidebar on p. 78. (If you do not have access to a digital image, find an image on a Web site, right click [Windows] or control click [Macintosh] to copy the image. In your document, position your cursor where you want the image to appear and use the* Edit > Paste *command from the main menu to insert the image.) After you have inserted the image, open the Format Picture dialog box by right clicking or control clicking on the figure with your mouse. Choose the Layout tab, and set the layout options to wrap text around the image. Experiment with different layout options on the page by dragging the image with your mouse to position it.*

4. *Insert a table by following the "How to Create and Format Tables" sidebar on p. 80.*

5. *Insert a chart or graph by following the "How to Create and Format Charts and Graphs" sidebar on p. 79. Once you have inserted the chart, open the Format Object dialog box by right clicking or control clicking on the chart with your mouse. Use the Layout tab to wrap text around the chart or graph, and then position it on the page by dragging the image with your mouse.*

6. *Create captions for the inserted images with text boxes by following the "How to Create and Format Text Boxes" sidebar on p. 55. After creating a text box, open the Format Text Box dialog box by right clicking or control clicking on the border of the text box with your mouse. Choose the Layout tab, and set the options to wrap text around the box. You can position the box below the image or chart by dragging it with your mouse. To eliminate the lines around your box, open the Format Text Box dialog box and choose the Colors and Line tab.*

PART THREE

Designing Documents

The design of your document reflects your purposes, your readers, and the setting in which the document will be read. It also reflects the type of document, or genre, you've selected. Genres have characteristic design features, such as the double-spaced lines and wide margins commonly used in academic essays and the columns, pull quotes, and illustrations often used in magazine articles. If you know the general characteristics of particular genres, you'll be prepared to apply your understanding of design principles and elements to the design of your document.

As you gain experience designing documents, you'll find that no single design satisfies the needs of every writing situation. Even if you are writing about the same topic for the same purpose, differences in audience and genre will strongly affect your design choices. Consider the designs of two documents—an academic essay and a flyer—about the same topic. Both documents address the topic of school reform in Colorado, draw on the same sources, make the same argument, and are written by the same writer, a college student whose mother teaches in a Colorado high school. However, the writer's decision to address two different audiences—a college writing instructor and the general public—leads to a different genre for each document. In turn, the characteristic design features of the two genres lead to strikingly different designs.

The academic essay (see Figure D) is designed like most academic essays: It has wide margins, plenty of line spacing, and a readable serif font. It uses

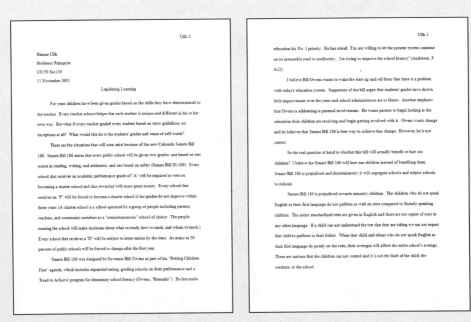

Figure D An academic essay opposing Colorado Senate Bill 186.

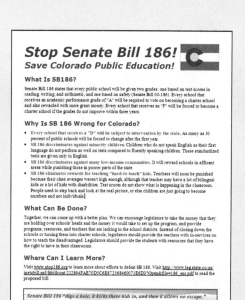

Figure E A flyer opposing Colorado Senate Bill 186.

neither illustrations nor color. Given its audience—a writing instructor who will evaluate it on the basis of clarity, organization, strength of argument, and use of evidence—it is a well-designed document.

A one-page flyer (see Figure E) that deals with the same information is designed quite differently. It uses color and graphics, bulleted lists, and a dramatic quotation set off from the rest of the text. Given its general audience—people who might see it at a public library or community center—its colorful headings and condensed listing of information make it an effective, visually appealing document.

As you gain experience writing and designing documents, you'll come to understand that genre plays an important role in shaping your design decisions. In Part Three we examine several common genres: academic essays, articles, brochures, flyers, multimedia presentations, and Web sites. As you look at examples of each, consider how differences among genres influenced the design decisions made by their authors.

CHAPTER 12

Academic Essays

The design of academic essays, in general, is neither flashy nor complex. Their most obvious design features—wide margins, readable fonts, and double-spaced lines—are intended to help their audience, typically instructors and classmates, read and review them. These features reflect the influence of the manuscript preparation guidelines provided by professional organizations such as the Modern Language Association. The overall goal of these guidelines is to simplify the task of editing a manuscript and preparing it for its transformation by the typesetter into a formatted document such as an article in an academic journal or a book. Because the primary focus of the writing assignments given by most college instructors has been on the written expression of the information and ideas in an essay, academic essays have tended to use images sparingly, if at all, and have rarely included color, shading, borders, or rules. Given recent changes in word processing technology, however, writers of academic essays are beginning to use these design elements more frequently.

12a Design Characteristics

With a few exceptions, the development of powerful document design tools in word processing programs such as Microsoft Word has done little to alter the overall design of academic essays. Those exceptions include the use of a high-quality laser or inkjet printer, the use of headings and subheadings, and the placement of illustrations in the body of the essay.

Headings and Subheadings   Headings and subheadings serve three functions in an academic essay. They help readers understand the organization of a document; they serve as transitional devices between sections and subsections of a document; and they add visual interest to what would otherwise be pages of unbroken text.

Learn about using headings and subheadings on p. 48.

Academic Essay Characteristics	
Purpose	Writers share their insights, ideas, and knowledge of a particular topic in a well-organized, well-supported, readable form.
Audience	Instructors are usually the primary readers of academic essays, although instructors will often ask writers to address a different audience, such as other students, politicians, parents, or members of a particular profession. In some cases, the choice of audience is left to the writer. Writers are instructed to thoroughly explain their points to their audience, support their points with appropriate forms of evidence, use a polite and reasonable tone, avoid slang, and acknowledge and cite sources.
Design	Academic essays typically use wide (one-inch) margins, single columns, and double-spacing. Essays sometimes use headings and subheadings, tables, charts, photographs, and drawings. Color is increasingly used in the design of essays, particularly for headings, subheadings, and illustrations.
Style	Although academic essays are often written in third-person voice (he, she, it, they), some instructors allow the use of first-person voice (I). Most essays use in-text citation format (MLA, APA, *Chicago* Author/Date), footnotes (*Chicago*), or endnotes (*Chicago*) to cite sources. The style is typically formal, with no slang. Some instructors do not allow the use of contractions.

Illustrations   Although the primary focus of academic essays is on the clear written expression of information and ideas, a number of college instructors now allow illustrations. The most commonly used illustrations are images (photographs or drawings), tables, graphs, and charts. Writers use illustrations to set a tone for a document, introduce and clarify main and supporting points, convince readers to accept an argument, and simplify the presentation of a complex concept. In many cases, illustrations are used to display complex information in an accessible form—information that would be difficult to follow in straight text.

Keep in mind that some instructors prefer that illustrations be kept to a minimum in essays, or even placed in an appendix. If you are uncertain about your instructor's preferences, ask for guidance.

Learn about using illustrations on p. 77.

12b Sample Academic Essay

The most important issues to consider when designing an academic essay are the needs of your readers. Most often, you'll think of your instructor as your reader. Occasionally, you'll also address your essay to your classmates, to a larger audience of people interested in your topic, or to the readers of a specific publication. The essay here, written by college freshman Gaele Lopez for his composition class, reflects his awareness of his instructor's expectations about line spacing, margins, documentation system, page numbers, and a title page. It also shows his understanding of his classmates and others who might be interested in his topic. Figures 12.1 through 12.5 show sample pages from Gaele's essay.

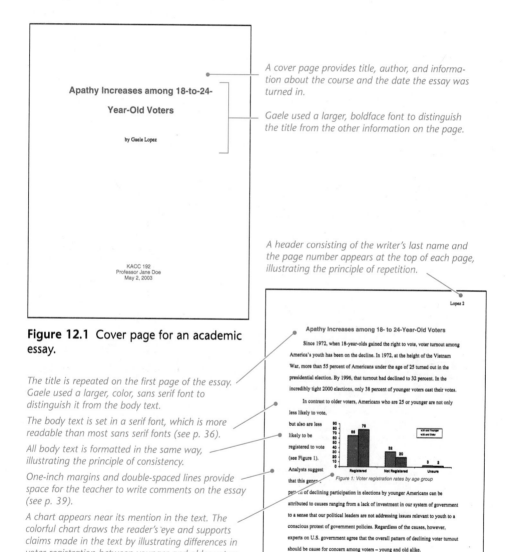

A cover page provides title, author, and information about the course and the date the essay was turned in.

Gaele used a larger, boldface font to distinguish the title from the other information on the page.

A header consisting of the writer's last name and the page number appears at the top of each page, illustrating the principle of repetition.

Figure 12.1 Cover page for an academic essay.

The title is repeated on the first page of the essay. Gaele used a larger, color, sans serif font to distinguish it from the body text.

The body text is set in a serif font, which is more readable than most sans serif fonts (see p. 36).

All body text is formatted in the same way, illustrating the principle of consistency.

One-inch margins and double-spaced lines provide space for the teacher to write comments on the essay (see p. 39).

A chart appears near its mention in the text. The colorful chart draws the reader's eye and supports claims made in the text by illustrating differences in voter registration between younger and older voters. Notice how text is **wrapped** around the chart (see p. 82).

Figure 12.2 First page of an academic essay.

Figure 12.3 Interior page of an academic essay.

A heading, formatted in blue and using a sans serif font that differs from the serif body font, calls attention to a shift in Gaele's argument.

A block quotation is set off by indenting the margins on both sides. Quotation marks are not needed for long quotations.

A table is set "inline" (see p. 82) in the text following the paragraph containing its mention in the text.

Figure 12.4 Table in an academic essay.

Gaele titles his reference page "Works Cited" per MLA style.

Gaele uses MLA format to cite his sources. Entries in the Works Cited list are double-spaced and have a hanging indent.

Figure 12.5 Works Cited page of an academic essay.

	Academic Essay Design Checklist
✔	Cover page with title, name, and course information
✔	Readable body font (example: 12 point Times New Roman; p. 35)
✔	Double-spaced lines (p. 39)
✔	Wide margins, one-inch or larger (p. 44)
✔	Consistent use of assigned documentation system (p. 29)
✔	Headers and footers use readable font distinct from body font (p. 48)
✔	If used, headings and subheadings formatted in fonts and colors that distinguish them from body text and show relative importance of heading levels (p. 48)
✔	If used, illustrations labeled and placed either within the text near relevant passages or in an appendix, according to instructor preferences (p. 81)

CHAPTER 13

Articles

The design of articles varies far more than the design of essays. In large part, this stems from the variety of publications in which articles appear: newspapers, magazines, Web sites, and newsletters, among others. Writers of articles need to consider several factors that affect design: the overall design of the publication in which they hope to place their article, the audience the publication addresses, the subjects typically written about in the publication, and the style used by other articles in the publication.

Article Characteristics	
Purpose	Writers provide information about an issue, an event, an individual, or a group.
Audience	Writers address the readers of a particular publication, such as *Time,* CNN.com, *National Review,* or Salon.com.
Design	The design of articles varies widely. Depending on the publication in which they appear, articles might use headings and subheadings, columns, sidebars, pull quotes, and illustrations.
Style	Style and voice reflect the standards of the publication in which the article appears and range from a serious tone with little room for the personal voice of the author to a breezy style filled with casual constructions.

13a Design Characteristics

Many of the design issues that apply to essays, including headings and subheadings, fonts, and illustrations (see p. 89), also apply to the design of articles. Several additional design elements should also be considered, including columns, sidebars, and pull quotes.

Learn about using columns on p. 44, sidebars on p. 56, pull quotes on p. 54, and drop caps on p. 56.

Columns   Newspaper and magazine articles, as well as a growing number of articles published on the Web, are often formatted in multiple columns. Columns can improve the readability of a document by limiting the physical movement of the eyes across the page. They can also simplify decisions related to the placement of illustrations and sidebars by dividing the page into areas into which illustrations and sidebars can be placed.

Sidebars   Sidebars display related information within an article in a way that shows it is not a central part of the article. Typically, the text of a sidebar is bordered and shaded so that it stands out from the main text of the article.

Pull Quotes   Writers use pull quotes to call attention to important facts or quotations, summarize a main or supporting point in a document, and entertain readers. Pull quotes are formatted differently from body text, usually in a larger font and often in a different color.

13b Sample Article

The article in Figures 13.1 and 13.2 (page 96), written by Christian Rangunton for the University of Texas at Arlington student newspaper, *The Shorthorn,* explores the experiences of international students at the university. It draws heavily on visual elements to set a mood, call attention to key points, and convey information. Like many newspaper articles, most of these visual elements are prominent on the opening page of the article and absent on the page on which the article is continued.

Article Design Checklist	
✔	Column layout appropriate for target publication and target audience (p. 44)
✔	Line spacing typically single-space (p. 39)
✔	Readable body font (example: 10 point Times New Roman; p. 35)
✔	Appropriate use of color (p. 66) and borders, shading, and rules (p. 74)
✔	Headings and subheadings formatted in fonts and colors that distinguish them from body text and show relative importance of heading levels (p. 48)
✔	Illustrations labeled and placed near relevant passages (p. 81)
✔	Optional elements: sidebars (p. 56), pull quotes (p. 54), marginal glosses (p. 54), and drop caps (p. 56).

A large headline in a color that contrasts with the main body text and the subheading. The subheading summarizes the main point of the article, allowing the reader to quickly decide whether to read the article.

Captioned photos and a background image of a passport add visual interest and information.

Like many newspaper articles, the article is formatted in columns (see p. 44).

Drop caps are used at the beginning and at two other points in the article.

A figure adds to the information provided in the text.

Byline set in all caps to differentiate it from main body text.

Figure 13.1 First page of a newspaper article. (*Source: The Shorthorn,* January 20, 2004, p. 3)

A brief headline and "continued from . . ." phrase indicate that the article began on a previous page.

The author's name and e-mail address appear at the end of the article, allowing readers with questions or reactions to contact the author.

Figure 13.2 Second page of a newspaper article in narrow columns. (*Source: The Shorthorn,* January 20, 2004, p. 7)

CHAPTER 14

Brochures

Brochures are typically used to provide information about an event or issue. Designed as compact, easy-to-carry documents, their distinguishing design feature is the use of folded sheets of paper to create pages. Most brochures consist of a single sheet of paper, printed on both sides, and folded one or more times. You'll also find brochures that are better described as booklets, with multiple pages of paper stapled together.

Brochure Characteristics	
Purpose	Writers provide information in a condensed, readable form about an issue, an event, an individual, or a group. Brochures are often used to encourage readers to learn more about a topic and typically provide contact information or a reference to other documents, such as a related Web site.
Audience	Writers address readers who are interested in or need to know about the topic.
Design	Brochures usually are compact enough to slip into a pocket, purse, or bag. They typically consist of a folded sheet of paper with a cover that clearly advertises the purpose and content of the brochure. Brochures tend to use headings and subheadings, illustrations, and color to create an attractive, easy-to-follow document.
Style	Style reflects the standards of the sponsoring organization and the characteristics of the target audience. Voice and tone range from informal to formal, and citation style varies.

14a Design Characteristics

The design options for brochures include decisions about fonts, text spacing and alignment, margins, columns, sidebars, pull quotes, and drop caps, as well as the use of illustrations, headings, and subheadings. The principles of placement and emphasis play important roles in brochure design.

Placement Because brochures use one or more folds, writers must anticipate which parts of the sheet of paper will serve as the cover, back page, interior pages, and so on. They must also be careful to position text and illustrations in a way that maximizes the effectiveness of each page of the brochure. In contrast to academic essays and articles, where illustrations are placed near their mention in the text, brochures often use "stand-alone" illustrations. In some cases, these illustrations provide information that isn't mentioned elsewhere in the brochure. In others, they serve solely to attract a reader's attention or to enhance the appearance of a cover or interior page.

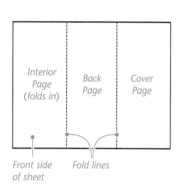

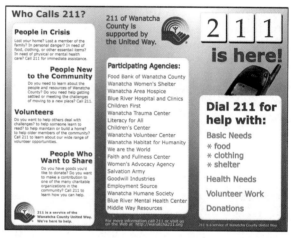

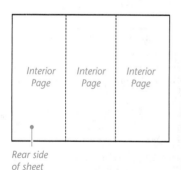

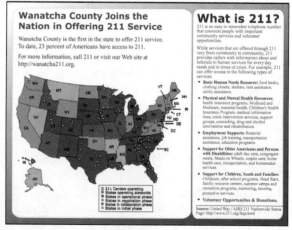

Figure 14.1 A two-fold design produces a six-page brochure.

Emphasis   Emphasis is also of critical importance, particularly for the cover of a brochure. If the cover is unattractive, or if the overall message is unclear, potential readers might not bother to look beyond it. Consider the cover of the Wanatcha County 211 brochure shown in Figure 14.1. While the brochure uses a design that provides a large amount of information to the reader, the cover is simple and informative. Potential readers will be able to determine its topic and purpose with a single glance.

Figure 14.2 Cover, back page, and interior fold of a brochure.

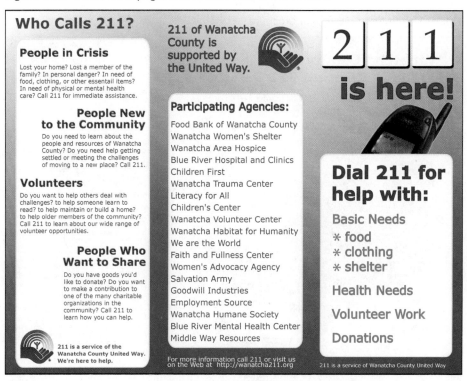

Interior Fold
- *The interior fold—the first page readers see—explains who will use the service and why they might use it, key questions readers might have if they are unfamiliar with the 211 service.*

Back Page
- *The back page of the brochure provides information about the sponsor, participating agencies, and contact information.*

Cover
- *The headline is clear and prominent, indicating the topic of the brochure and its content.*
- *The image of the telephone indicates that this is a telephone-based service.*
- *In bold, highly visible print, the primary functions and benefits of the 211 service are explained on the cover of the brochure.*

Similarly, the design and layout of the back and interior pages of a brochure can have a tremendous impact on readers' understanding. A writer's use of headings, illustrations, color, fonts, pull quotes, and other formatting elements will draw attention to particular areas of the pages of the brochure, highlighting important information and downplaying less important, secondary types of information, such as sponsoring organizations and contact information (see Figures 14.2 and 14.3).

Most brochures are created with one or two folds. The Wanatcha County 211 brochure uses a typical design: Two vertical folds are used to transform a letter-sized sheet of paper into a six-page brochure (see Figure 14.1).

Figure 14.3 Interior pages of a brochure.

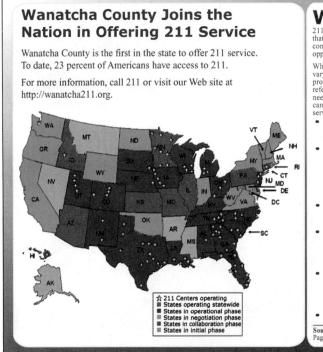

Wanatcha County Joins the Nation in Offering 211 Service

Wanatcha County is the first in the state to offer 211 service. To date, 23 percent of Americans have access to 211.

For more information, call 211 or visit our Web site at http://wanatcha211.org.

☆ 211 Centers operating
■ States operating statewide
■ States in operational phase
■ States in negotiation phase
■ States in collaboration phase
■ States in initial phase

What is 211?

211 is an easy to remember telephone number that connects people with important community services and volunteer opportunities.

While services that are offered through 211 vary from community to community, 211 provides callers with information about and referrals to human services for every day needs and in times of crisis. For example, 211 can offer access to the following types of services:

● **Basic Human Needs Resource:** food banks, clothing closets, shelters, rent assistance, utility assistance.

● **Physical and Mental Health Resources:** health insurance programs, Medicaid and Medicare, maternal health, Children's Health Insurance Program, medical information lines, crisis intervention services, support groups, counseling, drug and alcohol intervention and rehabilitation.

● **Employment Supports:** financial assistance, job training, transportation assistance, education programs.

● **Support for Older Americans and Persons with Disabilities:** adult day care, congregate meals, Meals on Wheels, respite care, home health care, transportation, and homemaker services.

● **Support for Children, Youth and Families:** Childcare, after school programs, Head Start, family resource centers, summer camps and recreation programs, mentoring, tutoring, protective services.

● **Volunteer Opportunities & Donations.**

Source: United Way / AIRS 211 Nationwide Status Page: http://www.211.org/faqs.html

Interior Pages
- *The interior pages provide more detailed information than the other pages in the brochure.*

- *Consistency is provided across the document through the use of headings set in a sans serif font, body text set in a serif font, and the use of rounded, yellow-bordered boxes.*

- *An eye-catching illustration provides information.*

- *Different-sized headings and subheadings, formatted in a color that contrasts with the body text, call attention to key points and indicate relative importance.*

14b Sample Brochure

The brochure in Figures 14.2 and 14.3, created as part of a service-learning project in a writing class, publicizes the new 211 service, which allows people to call a single number for help from health and human service agencies, to volunteer, and to donate time and money. The brochure draws heavily on visual elements, particularly on the cover, to attract the attention of potential readers. It also uses bulleted lists and headings to highlight important information.

Brochure Design Checklist
✔ Cover clearly conveys main point of the brochure
✔ Cover design draws the gaze of potential readers
✔ Overall design consistent across brochure panels (fonts, colors, rules, illustrations)
✔ Panels placed in appropriate locations to account for folding (p. 98)
✔ Readable body font (example: 10 point Times New Roman; p. 35)
✔ Headings and subheadings formatted in fonts and colors that distinguish them from body text and show relative importance of heading levels (p. 48)
✔ Lists often used to highlight important information (p. 53)
✔ Appropriate use of color (p. 66)
✔ Illustrations placed near the passages to which they refer, or stand alone (p. 81)
✔ Contact information and other relevant information included and easy to locate

CHAPTER 15

Flyers

Flyers are announcements printed on a single sheet of paper. Sometimes referred to as handbills, circulars, or broadsheets, they are usually intended for distribution to a wide audience, often through display stands and sometimes through direct mail. As in brochures (see p. 97), the first page of a flyer needs to convey a clear message that will appeal to prospective readers. Designing an attractive, informative front page, as a result, is critical.

Flyer Characteristics	
Purpose	Writers provide information in a condensed, readable form about an issue, an event, an individual, or a group. Like brochures, flyers are often used to provide essential information about a topic and typically provide contact information or a reference to other documents, such as a related Web site.
Audience	Writers address readers who are interested in or need to know about the topic.
Design	Flyers consist of a single sheet of paper printed on one or two sides. The first page is usually intended to catch a potential reader's eye and is likely to incorporate one or more illustrations, a headline, a limited amount of text, and, frequently, color. When a back page is used, it usually provides contact information and/or directions for learning more about the topic. The back page is likely to use headings and subheadings, illustrations, and color to create an attractive, easy-to-follow document.
Style	Style reflects the standards of the sponsoring organization and the characteristics of the target audience. Voice and tone range from informal to formal, and citation style varies.

15a Design Characteristics

Like brochures, flyers rely on effective use of headings and subheadings, bulleted and numbered lists, illustrations, colors, and borders and shading to emphasize their main points and provide information in a compact form.

Headings and Subheadings Flyers can vary significantly in the amount of information they attempt to convey. The flyer presented in Figure 15.1, for example, is typical of flyers that attempt to convey a great deal of information on a single page. Its use of headings helps the reader quickly scan the page to determine what the flyer is about.

Lists Flyers frequently use lists to quickly convey important information to readers. This flyer provides a list of upcoming events, formatted in bold to draw the reader's attention.

Illustrations Many flyers rely heavily on illustrations to attract attention. These illustrations are most effective when they also evoke or convey the main point of the flyer. The first page of the flyer in Figure 15.1 shows an attractive stand-alone illustration of a mountain valley. Combined with the title and a brief passage of text, the reader can quickly understand the main point of the brochure.

Flyers are successful only when they are picked up and read. To avoid the fate of most flyers—a quick trip to the recycling bin or burial under a pile of junk mail—take the time to create an attractive first page that clearly conveys the main point of the flyer.

15b Sample Flyer

Figure 15.1 shows the front and back pages of a flyer published by the Mountains and Trails Club, a student organization at a major western university. The flyer is designed to inform readers of upcoming trail building and maintenance events and to interest potential members in joining the club. As you review the flyer, consider how it uses formatted text, illustrations, colors, borders, and shading to clearly convey information about the club and its activities.

Figure 15.1
Front and
back page
of a flyer.

A heading and a subheading are set against a simple blue background and a striking image of the mountains. The cover uses an asymmetrical layout to suggest movement, illustrating the principle of balance (or, in this case, the lack of it). The design draws the reader's eye from the top of the page to the logo at the bottom of the page.

A heading set in white text against a blue background signals the main point of the document.

The triangular background used at the top of the page is repeated in the lower left corner, where it sets off the club logo.

2004 Trailbuilding Schedule

The Mountains & Trails Club sponsors monthly trailbuilding and maintenance activities. Meet at 7:30 am in front of the student center. Buses provide transportation to the site. Lunch is included. Please wear hiking boots, sturdy clothing, a hat, and gloves — and be sure to bring plenty of sunscreen.

April 17: Pingree Park
May 15: Cameron Pass
June 19: Glen Haven
July 17: Owl Canyon
August 21: Michigan Lakes
September 18: Rist Canyon

A simple list is set in colored, bold type that is larger than the body type elsewhere on the flyer, signaling to readers its centrality and importance.

A border around this passage sets it apart from other information on the page.

About the Mountains & Trails Club
The Mountains & Trails Club is funded by student fees. All University students, faculty, and staff are welcome to join. The 2004 annual meeting will be held on Thursday, April 8, at 7:00 pm in Student Center 303.

Contact information for the club.

Mountains & Trails Club
For more information:
MountainsTrails@university.edu
(990) 432-1234
http://www.university.edu/~mountains

Flyer Design Checklist

✔	First page clearly conveys main point of the flyer
✔	First page design draws the gaze of potential readers
✔	Overall design consistent across front and back page (fonts, colors, rules, illustrations)
✔	Readable body font (example: 10 point Times New Roman; p. 35)
✔	Headings and subheadings formatted in fonts and colors that distinguish them from body text and show relative importance of heading levels (p. 48)
✔	Lists often used to highlight important information (p. 53)
✔	Appropriate use of color (p. 66)
✔	Illustrations placed near the passages to which they refer, or stand alone (p. 81)
✔	Contact information and other relevant information included and easy to locate

CHAPTER 16

Multimedia Presentations

Multimedia presentations, sometimes referred to as PowerPoint presentations because they are so often created using Microsoft PowerPoint, consist of a series of slides that usually contain text and illustrations. Most multimedia presentations are designed to accompany and enhance the words of a speaker. When multimedia presentations are distributed as stand-alone documents, as is the case when they are presented on a Web site or distributed via CD or DVD, summaries of the speaker's words are sometimes provided through notes attached to each slide.

Multimedia Presentation Characteristics	
Purpose	Presenters typically offer information on a wide range of topics. Slides within the presentation usually provide a foundation on which the presenter builds with additional comments. Some slides may contain highly detailed information in the form of lists, tables, charts, graphs, images, animation, video, or audio.
Audience	Presenters address an audience who are interested in or need to know about a topic. Many presentations have two audiences: a primary audience who attends the presentation and a secondary audience who might read the presentation slides online or in print.
Design	Presentations consist of a linear sequence of pages, typically including an opening—or title—slide and one or more overview/introductory slides. Most presentations conclude with a summary slide. Page designs range from simple combinations of titles and lists to complex pages that incorporate illustrations and heavily formatted text. Presenters can highlight information though colors, fonts, tables, and an expanded range of illustrations, such as audio and video clips, animation, and links to online documents. Because many presentations are viewed on a computer or projection screen by a "live" audience, it is important to use legible fonts and illustrations.
Style	Style reflects the standards of the sponsoring organization and the characteristics of the target audience. Voice and tone range from informal to formal, and citation style varies.

16a Design Characteristics

A well-designed multimedia presentation engages the reader through an appropriate mix of textual information, images, audio, video, animations, and other forms of illustrations. In most cases, multimedia presentations serve as an accompaniment to a speech or presentation before an audience. The setting in which the presentation is displayed can have a profound impact on the design of the presentation. Writers of multimedia presentations intended for a "live" audience must consider a range of factors related to setting:

- The size of the screen on which the presentation will be shown, which can range from a small laptop LCD to a large television screen to a six-foot wide (or even larger) projection screen
- The size of the audience and the distance the audience members will be seated from the screen
- The power and clarity of available audio speakers, which can range from the built-in speakers of a laptop computer to a professional-quality sound system in an auditorium

Writers of multimedia presentations that are intended to be viewed by individual readers on a computer, as is the case when a presentation is distributed via the Web or on a CD or DVD, must also consider a range of factors related to setting:

- The speed and capability of the reader's computer
- The likely size and resolution of the reader's computer monitor
- The speed with which the reader's computer connects to the Internet, which can affect the ability to display audio, video, and animations

In addition to considering the impact of the presentation's setting, writers of multimedia presentations should consider design principles and elements that affect the readability and effectiveness of the individual slides in the presentation, such as color, headings and subheadings, bulleted and numbered lists, fonts and line spacing, and the use of digital illustrations and special effects.

Color Color can help set a mood in a multimedia presentation, typically through the use of a colored background and coordinated color scheme (for example, varying shades and hues of the same color or a related family of colors, such as earth tones or pastels). Color can also be used to call attention to important information on a slide. As you design a multimedia presentation, be judicious in your use of color—for example, avoid using brightly colored backgrounds that compete with information in the foreground of your slides.

Headings and Subheadings   Slides are most effective when they address a single concept or chunk of information and are clearly labeled with headings. Your headings should identify the main point of each screen. Subheadings, if used, should be simple and direct.

Bulleted and Numbered Lists   Most multimedia presentations make extensive use of bulleted and numbered lists. Lists allow you to present information concisely and are well suited to the limited size of a slide in a multimedia presentation.

Fonts and Line Spacing   As you would in a brochure, flyer, or Web site, use fonts and line spacing to draw the reader's eye to key points and important information and to enhance the readability of the document. Because your audience might be sitting some distance from the screen, display text on the slides in large, easy-to-read fonts. In general, you should avoid the overuse of text on a slide; use no more than six lines of six to ten words per line on each slide.

Digital Illustrations and Special Effects   In addition to images, charts, and tables, multimedia presentations can use a range of digital illustrations. Links on a slide can open a browser window containing a Web site, much as they can on a Web page. Similarly, links can open related documents, such as a spreadsheet or a word processing file. Animations and video can also be shown on a slide, and audio clips can be played automatically or with the click of a mouse. Multimedia presentation authoring software also supports the use of special effects, such as sound and visual transitions (such as a turning page, continuously playing background music, blinking or moving text, or the appearance of one page dissolving into the next). As you design your presentation, exercise restraint. Although these effects can gain the attention of your audience or set a mood, your audience can get tired of them. More important, overuse of special effects can distract your readers from the primary message of your presentation.

16b Sample Multimedia Presentation

Figures 16.1 through 16.5 show a selection of slides from a multimedia presentation about the impact of Senate Bill 186, a law passed by the Colorado state legislature in 2000 to reform public education in the state. As you review the slides, consider how color, headings and subheadings, bulleted lists, and illustrations help to clearly convey information about the impact of the bill.

A clear title, set in an easy-to-read sans serif font, contrasts well with the background and clearly presents the topic.

The opening slide uses an illustration that simultaneously focuses attention on children and evokes Colorado.

Figure 16.1 Opening slide of a multimedia presentation.

Slide titles are brief yet informative. Set in a sans serif font, this title is reversed against a light-colored bordered box, catching the eye.

A bulleted list and text formatting (bold, contrasting color, larger font size) highlight the key points and provide an overview of the bill.

Senate Bill 186: An Overview

- Became law on April 10, 2000.

- Public schools will be given an *Academic Performance Score* and a *Safety Score.*

- "Excellent" schools can become charter schools and receive additional funding.

- "Unsatisfactory" schools will become charter schools if no improvement occurs in 3 years.

Figure 16.2 Introductory slide of a multimedia presentation.

A chart shows the scores received by Colorado schools in 2003. The chart is clearly labeled using a font that can be read from a distance.

The source of the data used in the chart is identified, and a live Web link is provided.

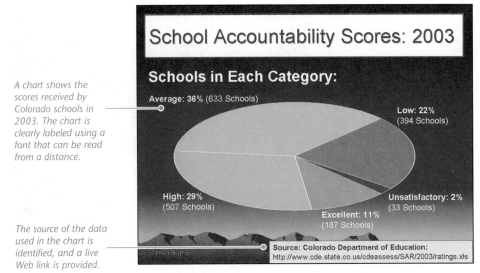

Figure 16.3 Multimedia presentation slide using a pie chart.

The slide provides a quotation that responds to a question posed in the header.

An icon is linked to a video interview with Patty Smith.

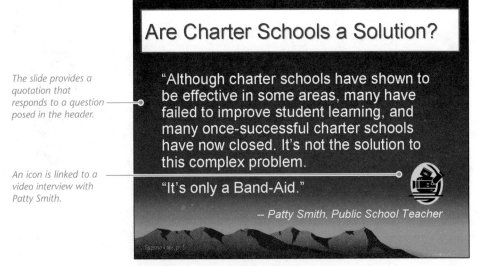

Figure 16.4 Multimedia presentation slide using a quotation.

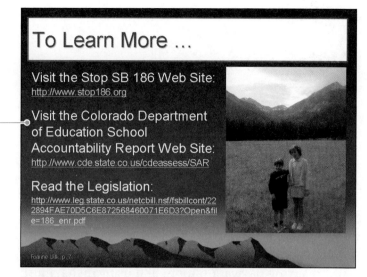

The final slide provides links to related Web sites and uses a photograph that focuses attention, once again, on Colorado's children. The Web links can be clicked to open the site in a browser.

Figure 16.5 Final slide of a multimedia presentation.

Multimedia Presentation Design Checklist
✔ Title page clear, uncluttered, and includes title of presentation
✔ Introductory pages provide clear overview of main points of presentation
✔ Overall design consistent across pages (placement of titles and text; use of fonts, colors, rules, illustrations)
✔ Readable heading font (example: 36 point Helvetica; p. 108)
✔ Readable body font (example: 24 point Helvetica; p. 108)
✔ Information presented in brief, readable chunks. Bulleted and numbered lists used whenever possible (p. 108)
✔ Appropriate use of color (p. 107)
✔ Illustrations, particularly charts, graphs, tables, and video, are easy to view at a distance
✔ If used, transitions between slides (dissolves, page flips) are not distracting
✔ If used, sound is audible and not distracting

CHAPTER 17

Web Sites

Web sites pose intriguing design challenges to writers. You must consider many of the design elements that are used in print documents, but you must also take into account the additional design options available to writers who publish online, such as selecting an organizational structure for a site, selecting navigation tools, and using digital illustrations. Most important, you must have some familiarity with the range of Web sites you can create, such as informative Web sites; articles for Web-based journals, magazines, and newspapers; business Web sites; personal home pages; and blogs, to name only a few of the genres that can now be found on the Web.

Web Site Characteristics	
Purpose	Writers offer information on a wide range of topics. Web sites usually provide broad overviews of the topic on the main pages of the site and add detailed information on related pages.
Audience	Writers address readers who are interested in or need to know about the topic. Given the diverse characteristics of individuals with access to the Web, writers must anticipate the needs of a far wider range of readers than is the case with most documents distributed in print.
Design	Web sites consist of linked pages, typically organized through a home page and navigational devices such as menus, tables of contents, indexes, and site maps. Web sites increasingly rely on designs similar to those found in magazines, with a heavy use of images and other illustrations. Web sites highlight information though colors, borders, shading, rules, fonts, tables, and an expanded range of digital illustrations, such as audio and video clips, animation, embedded programs and files (such as spreadsheets and word processing files), and links to information stored in databases.
Style	Style reflects the standards of the sponsoring organization and the characteristics of the target audience. Voice and tone range from informal to formal, and citation style varies.

17a Design Characteristics

The majority of design elements—such as fonts, line spacing, margins, columns, colors, borders, shading, illustrations, headings and subheadings, pull quotes, and drop caps—apply to both print and digital documents. Web sites and some types of digital documents, such as multimedia presentations, can use design elements not available for print documents, organizational structures impractical in print documents, and digital navigation tools. Because of this expanded range of design options, Web designers should approach Web site design in a manner that differs from their approach to the design of print documents.

Digital Design Elements

Additional design elements available to writers of digital documents include links, informational flags, pop-up windows, and digital illustrations.

Links   The ability to move from one document to another is the defining feature of the World Wide Web. As a designer, keep in mind that you are not limited to a sequential ordering of text. You can create complex documents in which the "next page" differs according to a particular reader's needs and interests. As you consider the design of a document that uses links, keep in mind the need to anticipate the options your readers are most likely to choose. If you want them to follow a particular path through your document (that is, to follow a specific sequence of pages), consider how you can use links to define that path.

Informational Flags   In many cases, your readers don't need to click on a link to learn something. Simply moving your mouse over links and images can cause an informational flag to pop up (see Figure 17.1). These flags can

Figure 17.1
Informational flag. A flag (in the yellow box) appears when the mouse cursor is placed on the photo on this Web page.
(*Source:* CNN.com)

Powell heading to Jerusalem for peace talks

From Matthew Chance
CNN
Tuesday, June 17, 2003 Posted: 11:36 AM EDT (1536 GMT)

GAZA CITY (CNN) -- U.S. Secretary of State Colin Powell will visit Jerusalem on Friday for meetings with Israeli and Palestinian officials, State Department officials said Tuesday.

The announcement came as Palestinian and Israeli leaders held talks in Gaza aimed at implementing

U.S. Assistant Secretary of State John Wolf, left, and Palestinian Prime Minister Mahmoud Abbas shake hands Tuesday in Gaza City.

help readers learn what will happen if they click on a link as well as provide information about images and other digital illustrations—information analogous to a caption in a print document. If you are working on a Web site using Microsoft Word, Microsoft FrontPage, or Macromedia Dreamweaver, you can create informational flags for links and images.

Pop-up Windows Sometimes called floating windows, pop-up windows appear in front of the current page you are viewing when you click on a link on a Web page (see Figure 17.2). Pop-up windows often function in the same way that endnotes or sidebars do in a print document. Instead of having to turn pages to view an endnote, however, you click on the link to open the window. Pop-up windows offer an important advantage over links that

Figure 17.2 Pop-up window. A pop-up window appears when the link "The Middle East 'Road Map'" is clicked in the Related box in an article on CNN.com. (*Source:* CNN.com)

replace the current page you are viewing with a new page: The page you are reading doesn't go away. This increases the likelihood that your reader will return to the page after opening the pop-up window. If you are working on a Web site using Microsoft Word, Microsoft FrontPage, or Macromedia Dreamweaver, you can create pop-up windows when you create a link by specifying that the page opens in a new window.

Digital Illustrations   Digital publications allow you to include a wider range of illustrations—such as audio files, video files, and animations—in your document. The Web also allows you to provide access to interactive content that is embedded directly on the page, such as data from a spreadsheet or a program that can help readers calculate the interest on a loan. Keep in mind, however, that factors such as the speed with which your readers connect to the Internet and the capabilities of your readers' computers might interfere with their ability to view digital illustrations. In addition, be wary of overusing digital illustrations and such special effects as animated images and blinking or moving text. When overused, these materials can annoy your readers or, worse, distract them from important information in your document.

Web Site Organizational Structures

Web sites typically use one or a combination of three organizational structures:

- Linear structure, similar to a series of pages in a book
- Hierarchical structure, in which pages are linked to each other according to their level in the hierarchy
- Interlinked structure, in which each page is linked to most or all of the other pages in the site

Each organizational pattern offers advantages for writers, depending on their specific purposes and their readers' needs and interests.

Linear Organization   A linear organization offers limited choices to a reader: forward and backward (see Figure 17.3). A linear, or sequential, organizational pattern is similar to that found in a book or a long essay. A feature article presented on the Web, for instance, might use a linear organization in which the home page is linked to the introduction, the introduction is linked to the first section of the article, and so on.

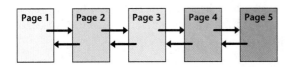

Figure 17.3 Web pages organized in a linear sequence.

Hierarchical Organization A hierarchical organizational pattern is frequently used for sites that provide categories of information, such as instructional, government, and commercial sites. Like a linear structure, however, a strict hierarchy offers limited navigational choices to readers: They can move up to a higher level in the hierarchy or down to pages lower in the hierarchy (see Figure 17.4). They cannot, however, move across the site to other pages that are at the same level in the hierarchy. Few sites, as a result, follow a strict hierarchical structure. Instead, they modify it through the use of navigation tools such as menus, tables of contents, and **cross links**—or links that move across levels or to other parts of the hierarchy.

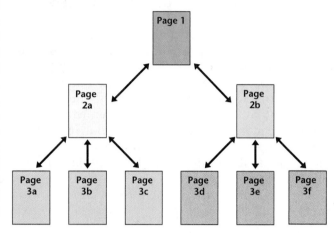

Figure 17.4 Web pages organized in a hierarchical structure.

Interlinked Organization In an interlinked site, it is possible to reach every other page in the Web site from a given page (see Figure 17.5). This organizational structure is used most effectively in smaller sites or in sites that use a navigational menu on each page. This organizational structure becomes difficult to support, however, when the site grows to more than a handful of pages. In a site composed of eight pages, for instance, each page would have seven links on it. In a site composed of 100 pages, each page would need to have 99 links on it. Sites that use a predominantly interlinked organizational structure often modify it by linking only to the most closely related pages and to major pages, such as the home page.

A Combined Organizational Structure Larger sites frequently use a mix of linear, hierarchical, and interlinked organizational structures (see Figure 17.6). A site that is organized in a more or less hierarchical structure, for instance, might incorporate linear and interlinked structures in some parts of the site. For example, the site might contain an introduction to some of the features on the site: Rather than providing links only back to the next higher page in the hierarchy, it would make more sense to provide links to the next page in the introduction.

Figure 17.5 Web pages organized in an interlinked structure.

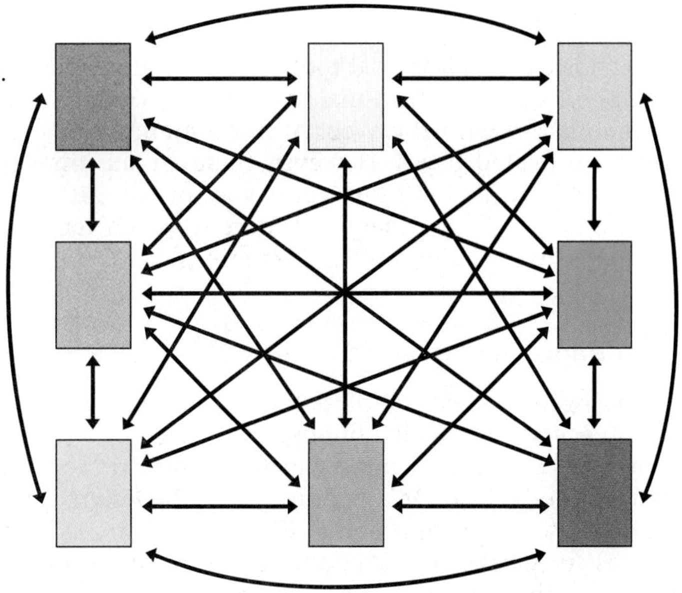

Figure 17.6 Web site using a combined organizational structure.

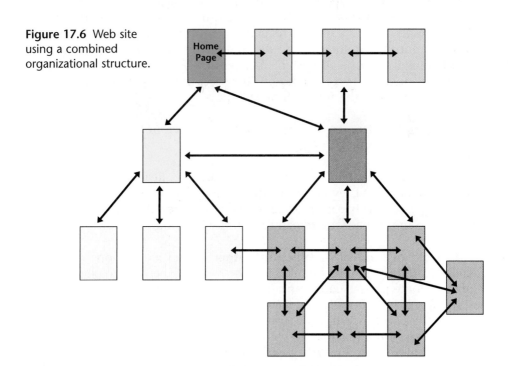

Navigation Tools

Your choice of navigational tools will depend on the size and complexity of your site, your organizational structure, and your knowledge of your readers' familiarity with the Web. At a minimum, you should provide links to and from related pages. However, there are advantages to providing additional support, including various types of navigation menus, navigation headers and footers, search tools, site maps, indexes, and tables of contents.

Learn about using navigation tools on p. 60.

Web Page Design Guidelines

Designing Web pages involves focusing on the overall look and feel of the pages on your site, which builds on the decisions you've made regarding its content, organization, and navigation tools. In the research writing tutorial *Writing the Web: HTML Coding and Web Design,* available at http://www .bedfordresearcher.com/manuals/html, you can read about 12 issues to consider as you design your Web site, including appropriate use of links and digital illustrations, page layout, and the development of a style guide for your site. The following principles underlie the design of an effective Web site.

1. Strive for a consistent design across your pages. Since one Web page is usually as easy to visit as another, avoid different designs on your pages. Different page designs can lead readers to think they've left your site and jumped to another. If you need to differentiate among your pages, use subtle variations in an overall design, such as differences in color, navigation aids, or placement of text on a page. Differences in your page designs should reflect differences in the function of each page.

2. Simple is better. Less is more. Don't try to cram too much on a single page.

3. Keep important information on the screen. Readers often jump to another Web page if they don't find what they're looking for on the screen. Although it's relatively easy to scroll down a page, few readers are willing to scroll down more than one screen to find the information they're seeking.

4. Avoid overuse of graphics and other digital illustrations. Graphics increase load time, the time it takes for a browser to open a Web page. A well-designed home page usually contains less than 40K of text and images. (To test the size of your home page, view the details of the HTML and image files used for the page. In Windows, use My Computer or Windows Explorer to view file sizes. On a Macintosh, view files in a folder.) In addition, research suggests that readers of Web pages are drawn to textual information as opposed to graphical information—a behavior that is strikingly different from readers' typical behaviors with print documents. Perhaps because so many Web sites use images largely as decoration rather than as sources of information in and of themselves (for example, news photographs, diagrams, and charts), readers typically look first at text on a Web page.

As you begin to design your Web site, browse the Web for sites with the same purpose as yours. Evaluate their site and page designs, making note of features and layouts that you might want to incorporate into your own site. Then, begin sketching designs on paper or in a graphics program. When you're satisfied with your design, get ready to create your pages.

17b Sample Web Site

Jenna Alberter, a student enrolled in an art history course, wrote the Web site in Figures 17.7 through 17.11 in response to an assignment to write about Baroque art. Selected pages are drawn from her site, including its home page, two representative content pages, a Works Cited page, and a contact information page. The work of designing the site consisted primarily of developing a single template that was used as the basis for all of the pages on the site. Once the template had been created, additional pages could be created simply by changing the title and inserting text and images.

A summary of the main point of the site is provided in text that stands out from the body text below it, illustrating the principle of emphasis.

A striking image of Vermeer's Girl with a Pearl Earring *is found on every page of the site.*

A side menu provides links to the major pages on the site.

Body text is formatted in Verdana, a sans serif body font designed for viewing on the screen. Every paragraph of body text is formatted in the same font and color across the site, illustrating the principle of consistency.

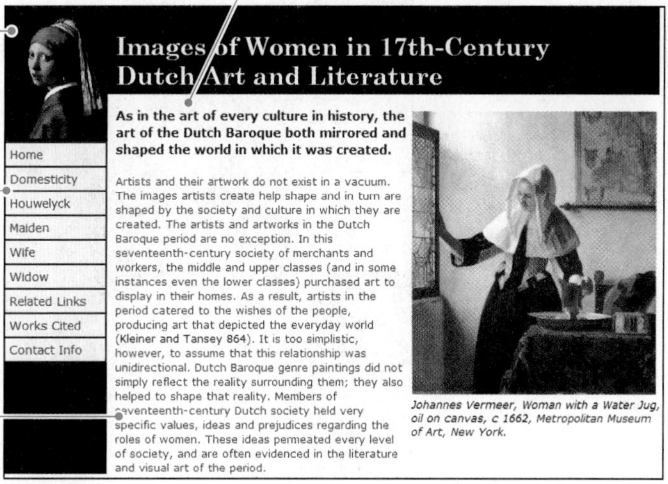

Images of Women in 17th-Century Dutch Art and Literature

As in the art of every culture in history, the art of the Dutch Baroque both mirrored and shaped the world in which it was created.

Home
Domesticity
Houwelyck
Maiden
Wife
Widow
Related Links
Works Cited
Contact Info

Artists and their artwork do not exist in a vacuum. The images artists create help shape and in turn are shaped by the society and culture in which they are created. The artists and artworks in the Dutch Baroque period are no exception. In this seventeenth-century society of merchants and workers, the middle and upper classes (and in some instances even the lower classes) purchased art to display in their homes. As a result, artists in the period catered to the wishes of the people, producing art that depicted the everyday world (Kleiner and Tansey 864). It is too simplistic, however, to assume that this relationship was unidirectional. Dutch Baroque genre paintings did not simply reflect the reality surrounding them; they also helped to shape that reality. Members of seventeenth-century Dutch society held very specific values, ideas and prejudices regarding the roles of women. These ideas permeated every level of society, and are often evidenced in the literature and visual art of the period.

Johannes Vermeer, Woman with a Water Jug, oil on canvas, c 1662, Metropolitan Museum of Art, New York.

Figure 17.7 Web site home page.

The titles on each page are formatted in Times New Roman, a serif font, contrasting with the sans serif body font. The title of the site is set in a smaller font above the title of each main page.

Following the principle of repetition, the menu appears in the same place on every page in the site.

An informational flag appears when the mouse cursor is placed on links on the site. This link brings the reader to the Works Cited page, increasing the usability of the site.

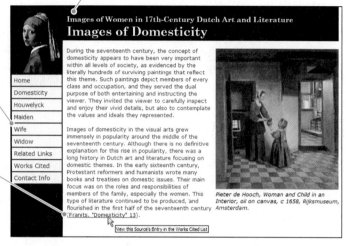

Figure 17.8 Web page on Baroque art.

Links are formatted in a color that differs from the main body text, helping readers easily locate text that is linked.

The layout of illustrations and captions is similar to that used in magazine articles, with text wrapping around the image.

The placement of the caption shows that it is related to the illustration. Source information is provided.

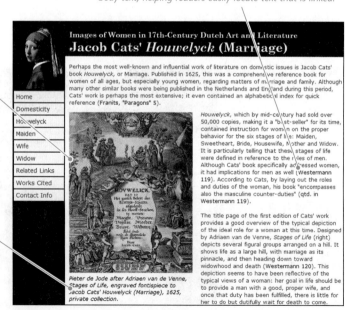

Figure 17.9 Web page on Baroque art.

The Works Cited page uses MLA style, which Jenna's teacher required. Hanging indents can be created using most Web editors. They can also be created using Cascading Style Sheets (CSS).

Links to online sources help readers easily open and review them. The pop-up flag lets readers know they can visit the site by following the link.

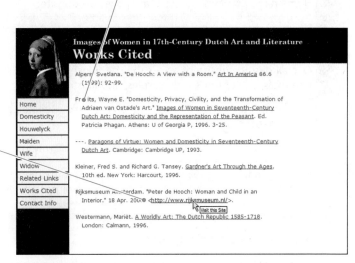

Figure 17.10 Online Works Cited page using MLA style.

The contact information page allows readers to get in touch with the author of the site and provides information about the site's origins and purpose.

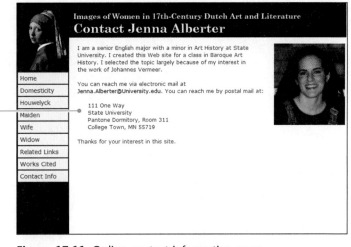

Figure 17.11 Online contact information page.

Web Design Checklist	
✔	Organizational structure consistent with the purpose of the site and the needs/expectations of readers
✔	Home page provides links to main pages on the site
✔	Home page and main pages provide navigation tools appropriate for readers of site
✔	Overall design consistent across the site (placement of titles, text, and navigation tools; use of fonts, colors, rules, and illustrations)
✔	Information presented in brief, readable chunks. Bulleted and numbered lists used whenever possible (p. 53)
✔	Readable body font (example: 12 point Times New Roman; p. 35)
✔	Headings and subheadings formatted in fonts and colors that distinguish them from body text and show relative importance of heading levels (p. 48)
✔	Informational flags used to help readers understand links and images
✔	Appropriate use of color (p. 66)
✔	Illustrations placed near the passages to which they refer (p. 81)
✔	Images are kept as small (in kilobytes) as possible, subject to concerns about clarity of images (p. 118).
✔	Contact information and other relevant information included and easy to locate

Resources for Document Design

The following Web sites provide guidance in designing print and digital documents.

Document Design

Typography and Page Layout	http://www.typography-1st.com/typo/txt-lay.htm
All Good Things Typography	http://www.redsun.com/type/
HCIRN Design Documents	http://www.hcirn.com/tutor/docs
EServer TC Library	http://tc.eserver.org
Bedford Researcher Web Development and Document Design Links	http://www.bedfordresearcher.com/links/web.cfm
Using Your Word Processor	http://www.bedfordresearcher.com/manuals/wp
Beyond BIU: Designing Documents with Microsoft Word	http://dept.seattlecolleges.com/tlc/resources/word.html

Web Design and Development

Web Style Guide	http://www.webstyleguide.com
Web Page Design for Designers	http://www.wpdfd.com
Mike Markel's Web Design Tutorial	http://www.bedfordstmartins.com/markel_tutorial
Writing the Web: HTML Coding and Web Design	http://www.bedfordresearcher.com/manuals/html
useit.com: Jakob Nielsen's Web site	http://www.useit.com
About.com on Web Design	http://webdesign.about.com
HTML Help by the Web Design Group	http://www.htmlhelp.com
Web Site Tips for Designers	http://www.websitetips.com/design

Desktop Publishing

About.com on Desktop Publishing	http://desktoppub.about.com
DesktopPublishing.com	http://desktoppublishing.com
Introduction to Desktop Publishing	http://writing.colostate.edu/references/documents/desktop_publishing

Graphic Design

About.com on Graphic Design	http://graphicdesign.about.com
Ideography: "But I Can't Draw!"	http://www.ideography.co.uk/drawing/download.html
Graphic Design: USA	http://www.gdusa.com

Information Design and Information Architecture

The Society for Technical Communication Information Design Special Interest Group	http://www.stcsig.org/id/
InfoDesign: Understanding by Design	http://www.informationdesign.org/
EServer TC Library: Information Design	http://tc.eserver.org/dir/Information-Design
Information Architecture Tutorial	http://hotwired.lycos.com/webmonkey/design/site_building/tutorials/tutorial1.html

Acknowledgments

Figures B, C, 7.8: Claudia Wallis, "Guess What F Is For? Fat" from *Time* (September 15, 2003). Copyright © 2003. Reprinted with the permission of Time, Inc.

Figures 1.1, 1.2, 17.8: Peter de Hooch, "Woman and Child in an Interior" (oil on canvas, c. 1658, Rijksmuseum, Amsterdam).

Figures 1.1, 1.2, 17.7: Johannes Vermeer, "Woman with a Water Pitcher" (New York, Metropolitan Museum of Art). Oil on canvas; 18 x 16 in. (45.7 x 40.6 cm) Marquand Collection, Gift of Henry G. Marquand, 1889 (89.15.21).

Figure 1.3: Romesh Ratnesar, excerpt from "Al-Qaeda's New Home" from *Time* (September 15, 2003). Copyright © 2003 by Time, Inc. Reprinted with permission. Includes Rabih Moghrabi, photograph of Al-Qaeda warning (AFP/Getty Images; #2411022). Reprinted with permission.

Figure 1.4: Paul Miller, "New building, walkway grace campus" from *Comment Newsletter* (September 5, 2002). Photo by Paul Miller. Reprinted with the permission of Paul Miller, Colorado State University.

Figure 1.5: Three (3) screenshots from "Across the Disciplines" Web site, http://wac.colostate.edu/atd/911/. Reprinted with permission.

Figure 2.1: Screenshot from "The Martin Luther King, Jr. Papers Project at Stanford University" Web site, http://www.stanford.edu/group/King. Photographs of Dr. Martin Luther King, Jr. appear courtesy of Intellectual Properties Management, Atlanta, Georgia, as Manager for the Estate of Dr. Martin Luther King, Jr.

Figure 2.2: Photograph of NYC firefighters silhouetted against ruins of the World Trade Center from Nancy Gibbs, "Life During Wartime" from *Time* (September 15, 2003). Copyright © 2003 by Time, Inc. Reprinted with permission.

Figure 2.3: Peter Fish, excerpt from "Horse Haven" from *Sunset* (July 2003). Copyright © 2003 by Time, Inc. Reprinted with permission.

Figure 2.4: Screenshot from National Public Radio Web site, http://www.npr.org/display_pages/features/feature_1503606.html. This material is used with the permission of National Public Radio, Inc. Any unauthorized duplication is strictly prohibited.

Figure 2.5: American Lung Association of Texas, screenshot from Why You Should Quit Web site, http://www.texaslung.org/programs/tobaccocontrol/whyquit.htm. Copyright American Lung Association of Texas, http://www.texaslung.org. Reprinted with permission.

Figure 2.6: Diagram, "Biological activity, Growth, Biomass" from Pascal M. Baillod and Gary O. Martini, "La photosynthèse source de vie comme diagnostique de l'environnement" from APTE Association Web site, http://www.apte.net/biotech/bioworld-f.htm. Reprinted with permission.

Figure 3.2: Phi Beta Kappa, "In This Issue" (table of contents) box, and Deborah Morello, photograph, "Rye Schwartz-Barcott, trying a dance step with Joy Festo, in Nairobi, Kenya..." both from *The Key Reporter* (Spring 2003): 1, the quarterly newspaper of the Phi Beta Kappa Society. Reprinted with permission.

Figure 3.3: Sidebar in an article from *PC World* (June 2003), p. 52. Reprinted with permission.

Figure 7.2: Noam Scheiber, "Exit Poll: The people who really run the Democratic Party" from *The New Republic* (February 24, 2003). Copyright © 2003 by The New Republic LLC. Reprinted by permission of *The New Republic*.

Figure 7.3: Screenshot of Salon.com Web site with excerpt from David Bauder, "The Clash, Elvis Costello join rock Hall of Fame" (March 11, 2003). Reprinted with permission.

Figure 7.9: Excerpt from *Real Simple* (April 2003): 226. Copyright © 2003 by Time, Inc. Reprinted with permission.

Figure 8.3: Screenshot of The New Republic Online home page, http://www.tnr.com (July 3, 2004). Copyright © 2004 by The New Republic LLC. Reprinted by permission of *The New Republic*.

Figure 10.1: Excerpt from Dawna Duncan, "Tayson Writes to Free a Voice" from *The Freestone* (Spring 1998), Colorado State University, Department of English. Reprinted with permission.

Figures 13.1, 13.2: "Scene" page and article continuation from *The Shorthorn* (January 20, 2004): 3, 7. Reprinted with permission.

Figures 17.1, 17.2: "Powell Heading to Jerusalem for Peace Talks" from CNN.com Web site. Reprinted with permission.

Index

About the Author

Mike Palmquist, Professor of English and University Distinguished Teaching Scholar at Colorado State University, is recognized nationally for his work in computer-supported writing instruction and, in particular, for his work in designing Web-based instructional materials to support writing. His most recent Web-based projects are Writing@CSU (http://writing.colostate.edu), the writing center Web site at Colorado State University, and the WAC Clearinghouse (http://wac.colostate.edu), the leading site for communication across the curriculum.

Palmquist has directed Colorado State University's composition program for six years and has codirected the university's Center for Research on Writing and Communication Technologies for more than a decade. He is the author of *The Bedford Researcher*, as well as numerous articles and essays on writing and teaching with technology and writing across the curriculum. He is the 2004 recipient of the Charles Moran Award for Distinguished Contributions to the Field, which recognizes "exemplary scholarship and professional service to the field of computers and writing."

Figures by Genre

Academic essays

Articles

Web documents